Living Cheaply With Style

Ernest Callenbach

RONIN Publishing
Berkeley, CA
www.roninpub.com

Living Cheaply With Style, Second Edition
ISBN: 1-57951-014-0

Self-Mastery Series #3

Published by
Ronin Publishing, Inc.
Post Office Box 522
Berkeley, California 94701
www.roninpub.com

Cover Design, original: Brian Groppe
Cover Design, revised: Judy July, Generic Typography
Printer: Bertelsmann

This book evolved from previous works by the author:
Living Poor With Style
Bantam/Straight Arrow, 1972
The Ecotopian Encyclopedia
And/Or Press, 1980
Living Cheaply with Style
Ronin Publishing, 1993

U.S. Library of Congress Catalog number 00-104-338

Printed in the United States of America

Dedication

To all who think for themselves
and stay conscious of the
choices that shape their lives . . .

To all who know in their bones
that enough is enough, and want
to figure out how much that is . . .

To all who understand that thrift,
generosity, and resourcefulness mimic
nature and help preserve the Earth . . .

To all who wish to survive
with grace, humor, imagination,
and a little help from their friends . . .

Other Books by Callenbach

Bring Back the Buffalo!
A Sustainable Future for
America's Great Plains

Ecotopia

Ectopia Emerging

Ecology
A Pocket Guide

EcoManagement

Publisher's Lunch

Humphrey the Wayward Whale

Table of Contents

Table of contents continued

Introduction

The aim of this book is to equip you to live a better life—more relaxed, more confident, more resilient, more loving, more thoughtful, more satisfying, more genuinely stylish with less money. The first step is to focus on what's really important in life—a life that's abundant in what matters. By "living cheaply" we keep cash in its proper subordinate place—living economically, ingeniously, creatively, and with what we might call spiritual efficiency or even elegance.

If you've traveled in foreign countries where the average cash income is far lower than yours, you've probably noticed that people do not seem unhappier than people where you live. In fact, even people who we would consider to be desperately poor often live cheerful and productive lives. This contrast tells us that the ability to buy a lot of goods is not the critical factor in making human beings happy.

> Being frugal,
> one has
> *abundance.*
> —LaoTzu

What is critical is our attitude about what makes us happy. Take a moment to appreciate the potent pleasures of your senses, to which every fragrant flower, every birdsong, every sight of billowing grass or trees, every loving touch contribute mysterious and moving experiences. Pay more attention to people, both those important in your life and those just passing through; they respond in wonderful ways to being carefully listened to, looked at, shared with, invited. Observe the creatures and plants we cohabit the planet with—they never shop, and yet they live gracious, beautiful, stylish lives.

Style is Being Who You Are

You live with style when you live in a self-determined and original way that's authentic for you, when you do things you enjoy because you enjoy them. You live with style when you keep your mind free to invent ways of thinking, feeling, and doing that suit *you*. You live with style when you rely on your own practiced judgment.

Style is a matter of independence, even rebellion; it's not fashion, which is only a matter of commercially fostered fads. True style comes from knowing who you are.

Modern life presents us with a paradoxical living environment. We praise independence of spirit but we're sheep in our consumer behavior. Living with style means being your own person. Part of the pleasure of living cheaply with style is to share your tricks and achievements with others, to build a counter-culture in which human beings can live more comfortably and satisfyingly, and to help make modern life saner and more humane—for ourselves and for those who come after us.

If you're an independent spirit, find friends who are also. We all need people to confide in, to rely on in times of trouble and help when they're in trouble, to laugh and cry with, and to share our thoughts. It's wonderful to have friends to try your new ideas out on, to bat reactions back and forth, to engage in new projects with.

Honor "Enoughness"

Until recently, being frugal was honored. People were proud of doing things economically, of not wasting, of making do with what was available. This book will help you to be thrifty in ways your grandparents would find familiar.

It's a fascinating challenge to see what is the absolute minimum you can lead a good life on—and it's a lot less than most people imagine. It's not necessary to be a fanatic, only thoughtful. Once your necessities of food, shelter, and medical care have been met, an honest evaluation of your experience will almost certainly show that, beyond a certain point, most added expenditures bring decreasing returns of satisfaction. After that point, your precious life's time—the only resource you're born into the world with—is being used to procure things that leave you restless and disappointed or may actually decrease your real happiness. If you learn what "enough" is for you, you'll keep better control of your time and yearn less after having more stuff.

Competence

When people used to live in the country or in small towns, repair and maintenance services were scarce. People had to develop competence and ingenuity—the ability to understand how things work, to use things efficiently, take care of them, repair them when needed, or figure out alternatives if they broke down. In our urbanized consumer society, we've come to depend on artifacts whose workings we don't understand and which we can't fix. This book is aimed at rebuilding your competence with information you need to develop skills that are essential to survive comfortably on modest amounts of money.

Even questions of diet involve competence. We became a nation of fast-food eaters and lost a sense of healthy eating. Competence requires confidence; confidence in our own abilities to learn and cope is the route to competence. Lean as little as possible on experts, whether they're plumbers or psychotherapists. Everybody in so-called primitive societies knows how to build houses, dispose of wastes, find and grow food, prepare it, deal with common diseases and accidents, give birth, care for children, and so on. If our future is to be secure, we need to achieve at least halfway similar levels of competence in our modern circumstances. This book gives you a handy and compact source for competence-building bits of information, and a framework for understanding the bits you accumulate on your own.

Think for Yourself!

Conventional ways of doing things *may* make sense, but often they make sense mainly to the people who profit from them and you'd be better off to find or invent another way. Be critical and analytical about information. Even apparently authoritative sources may contain large or small errors, and a smart person is constantly cross-checking and verifying things. This is especially true in the age of the Internet, when vast amounts of questionable information shout at us from millions of web sites. It helps to remember that most net information is there for commercial purposes: it's trying to sell you something.

Live cheaply with style and save the Earth.

The simple act of consuming less is probably the most radical step you can personally take to save the Earth.

Employ the Green Principle:

Buy Less!

1

OVERCOME MONEY PHOBIA

It is amazing how many people have hang-ups about money—hang-ups that can reduce your freedom and keep you poorer than you need to be. If you don't know how to drive your car, you will run into trees. If you don't know how to manage money, you'll run into debt.

It's important to get control of your money. If your money controls you with debts and hounding bill collectors, for example, you have diminished freedom. A realistic relationship with money is a major key to living with less stress and more style. It takes strength of character and using your head. For instance, you're swimming upstream against a fierce current if you carry heavy credit-card debt. Once you get your money life in order, you can relax and pay attention to increasing the style in your life.

Dealing with money takes careful planning because it doesn't take care of itself and when ignored it has a way of disappearing. To get on top of your money you need to have a clear picture of where your money is coming from and where it's going. This takes some work, but the payoff is increased freedom, relief from needless stress—and usually extra money.

Learn to Handle Money

You can't be a good manager of your money when you are ignorant. Shed your fears and misconceptions about money and learn to use it to your best advantage. It's smart to take a course, read books and articles, watch business news shows. Retread your thinking so that you look upon hearing financial discussions and information as an opportunity to learn incredible secrets, instead of something boring and horrible that gives you a headache. Even if you don't understand it, just let it filter through your mind and a little will stick, making it easier for you to learn.

Think Investment

Don't always look at things in terms of what is the cheapest. Instead, weight all the factors to make the best buy—which is sometimes the more expensive alternative. For example, it might be smarter to buy a more expensive but higher quality wool coat that you will wear for years, than a less expensive one that will barely last the season. On the other hand, if you are rough on your clothing or you'll be in the winter climate for only a short time, a cheaper coat of lesser quality might be right. Wear it for two months and discard it.

Investment generally means that you expect the purchase to increase in value. Let's say that you are shopping for a dining table. You can probably purchase a cheap new table for about the same price as a better used table. Which is the better investment? The cheap new one is going to look good for a while, but it's made of laminated and glued plywood. Its value will drop—*depreciate*. Now consider the better used table. Its materials are probably solid wood. In fact, it may be a "near" antique. If you're clever and take time, you can probably buy an antique, or soon-to-be-antique for the same price or even less than the new, lower quality table. The bonus is that the used table is an investment and actually grows in value—*appreciates*—over time.

The wonderful thing about "thinking investment" is that with this special eye you can fill your home and your closet with wonderful, inexpensive things that will be worth more in ten or fifteen years than they are today. The cheap but new item probably won't even last anywhere near that long.

Attend Free Financial Seminars

Whenever there is a change in the tax laws, and at certain times of the year like at tax time or the end of the year when people are doing last-minute tax transactions, savings and loans, banks, brokerages, and other financial institutions often have free financial seminars. These seminars teach you about Roth IRAs, T-Bills, CDs, bonds, mutual funds, and other financial tools as well as retirement planning. It is smart to go to these seminars. You often get a free continental breakfast or canvas bag. All you have to do is sit and let them feed you information. But leave your checkbook at home because they will probably try to sign you up for something.

Look upon financial information as secret keys. Actually, the rich live more cheaply than you realize and they live in much finer style. If you can find out some of their financial secrets you can use and implement them—then you can live very cheaply and very much in style.

Budget

One way to stretch money is to divide it into weekly amounts, and then spend only that amount. This is the only reliable way to keep from borrowing against the future. The object is to spread your expenses out as evenly as you can. If you need something that is not covered in your budget, save up by scrimping this week, so you do not have to raid your savings. If you come out at the end of a week with a surplus of money, you can add it to your savings or treat yourself to a luxury you've been wanting.

Save First

Put aside the savings first, then budget for the week. Traditional advice is to strive to set aside a minimum of 10% of your income as savings. This would mean that the first bill you pay is a check to yourself in the amount of 10% of your income. Promptly deposit it into your savings account and pat yourself on the back. If you don't make the 10% mark, don't give up. Save what you can—even if it's only a few dollars. Develop a habit of saving. Think of it as the drip technique. Even a few dollars saved every week can eventually overflow your cup.

A lot of people have great intentions to save, but don't. Their money just seems to disappear. Yet, almost everyone has a little money that they can shave off their budget and set it aside as a nest egg. When it comes to savings, you are probably your own worst enemy. Sometimes you must trick yourself.

Keep Savings Separate

Keep your savings separate from your daily living money. For one thing, checking accounts don't usually pay interest. You want to keep savings in an interest-bearing account, not only for the interest paid this month, but more important, for compound interest, which causes your money to grow faster the longer it is in the account.

Another important reason to not keep your savings in your checking account is that it is all too easy to spend it. If you make a mistake in your accounting you can spend it by mistake. You can spend it on an impulse.

Put Hurdles in Your Path

One strategy to keeping your savings safe is to put hurdles between yourself and your savings account. Open a savings account in a different financial institution. Write a check to yourself, just like paying a bill, and deposit it in your special "distance" account. Then, if you desperately need money you can get it, but it's out of your reach for impulse buying. Make depositing easy. You can usually mail in deposits to your savings account, so mailing off your savings check is as simple as paying other bills.

If you don't keep your savings account in the same financial institution as your checking account, you won't get into the habit of using your savings as overdraft protection for the checking. All it takes is one impulse buy, or one big bookkeeping error to drain your savings. If you want to use a savings account for overdraft protections, instead of a credit card, then set up a special account with only $500 or $1000 in it.

Another potential hazard of using your savings account for overdraft protection, is in the terrible situation where someone gets and successfully uses your checks. Guard all your financial information, including your Social Security number. Automatic deposits of Social Security checks, or other income, avoids the risk of somebody raiding your mailbox.

Use Numerous Accounts

Another technique is to use numerous accounts. As you succeed in building your savings and your balance grows, it is easy to think you are in fat city and to get lazy in your resolve to save religiously. When you use several accounts, you can have a lot of savings, yet each account's balance looks modest. The multiple account approach is especially good when you are saving for different things, like a child's education, Christmas and birthday gifts, vacations, special dental work, and so forth. Here you place certain monies you obtain into special accounts. For example, you might put 10% of your pay check into the account for your child's education—because that is the biggest debt and the most important to you. You might put all surplus money you save from groceries into your vacation account—because a trip to Hawaii is the reward you will give yourself and your family for living cheaply.

The number of accounts you can have is unlimited. Savings accounts rarely have fees. You can build up an account to a pre-determined amount, say $3000, then move that into a longer-term, higher-interest-paying account or "certificate of deposit" (CD), for example.

2

Establish Credit

Credit is the ability to borrow money from banks, stores, credit-card companies, or loan companies when you need it. But the best time to establish credit is when you *don't* need it. Then later, it will be available if you face an emergency or decide to make a purchase for which you don't want to tie up all your funds.

One good strategy is to select a card that has a low annual fee and the lowest available interest rate on unpaid balances. Sometimes, just asking for it on the phone will get you a lower rate. Use your card for a couple of small purchases and make payments promptly. Then put the card in your drawer and use it only for rare and specific purposes.

Credit-rating agencies keep track of your credit history. Some companies report every late payment, so you need to be careful. If you ever apply for a home loan, for example, you will have to write an explanation of each late payment! When a blot is laid on your credit—and blots are practically inevitable because of reporting errors—it's worth the trouble to find out why and take action to repair your credit history.

Beware of the "Free" Report

Credit reporting agencies make money by collecting information about your financial situation and selling it. They are most interested in negative information—late payments, too much debt, failure to pay.

If you are denied credit, consumer protection laws require that the company denying you credit tell you the reason and which credit reporting agency gave them information. Credit agencies offer a "free" report to persons who have been denied credit. Watch out, because this is a trap.When you request the "free" report, you have unwittingly informed the credit reporting agency that you have been denied credit! Then they add this negative information to your record. Never get the free report. Instead, contact the credit reporting agency and purchase a report of your credit which costs around $8.50 to $15.

When you receive your report, it will provide you with specific instructions on how to challenge or correct incorrect information on your report. You are permitted to write a brief explanation of each "black mark." Always send an explanation. It might be that your payment was lost in Christmas holiday mail, which caused it to arrive late, for example.

Maintain a Paper Trail

If you are billed incorrectly, call and question the billing. Ask the credit card billing clerk to note on your record that you called and the reason you will not be paying a particular amount. Then send a follow up letter—and keep a copy. Keep a note of whom you spoke to, the date you spoke, and what was promised, just in case they don't follow through or some other mix-up occurs. Not paying a "disputed" amount is not supposed to be reported to credit agencies. Such disagreements are supposed to be resolved within 90 days of your complaint.

Don't Apply for Too Much Credit

Every time you apply for credit, the company giving the credit "runs a credit check" on you. These queries are added to your credit history. If you are just shopping around for a car, for example, be careful to *not* allow the salesman to get financial data on you because that dealer may run a report on you. You go to the next lot and they may do the same thing. Before you know it, your credit history is damaged simply because three or four auto dealers merely asked about your credit. Maybe you didn't buy a car at all! Be careful about this. Later, if you apply for a home loan, you will have to explain each of these requests for your credit report.

Another danger is having too many credit cards. Credit cards are so easy to get that many people have several cards in their drawer that they are not using and that have zero balances. Formulas are used that factor in the number of cards issued in your name; the more you have, the lower your rating. Lenders, especially home loan lenders, use these ratings to determine the interest rate they offer you. Lower rating, higher interest rate.

Use Credit Cards Wisely

There are many advantages to using credit cards, but as we all know, they can be very dangerous. They are seductive, making it easy to overspend so that you find yourself in a prison of escalating credit card debt.

Reduce Credit-Card Debt

A critical financial step is to pay off your credit-card debts. Interest on a credit-card balance eats up both your present and your future. The basic step out of the financial hole is hard but simple. Steadily and persistently save enough from regular and impulse expenses to pay down your cards. The feeling of having credit debt under control is wonderful! If your credit cards have gotten the better of you, it's smart to get a professional debt reduction counselor to help you.

Use Discipline

The single most important thing you can do when using credit cards is exercising your discipline. It is easy to get carried away on a buying spree, without realizing how much you have spent.

Leave the Card Home

Don't carry the card with you. When you don't have the card with you, you can't use it impulsively. If there is an important purchase to be made, you can easily get the card and take it to the store.

Be Selective

Avoid using your card for every purchase because this is the road to financial disaster. Use it selectively. One standard is to use the credit card for large purchases, like big appliances, and emergency situations, like car repairs.

Make a Pay Back Plan

Think of yourself as being your own lender when you use your credit card. Be demanding of yourself. Most important, set up a payback plan before making the purchase. Say you buy a computer for your business or pay for a large car repair. Write out on paper over how many months you will spread your payments. Make sure to add in the cost of the interest you must pay to the card company. Then determine how much you will pay each month. Be realistic; make sure it will fit your budget.

Pay Early

The newest hazard of credit cards is the "late fee" which is usually $29 or more, and billed to your account if your payment is even one day late. Often there is a several day delay between when your payment arrives and when it is applied. So to be safe, you should send credit card payments about two weeks before their due date. If you are charged a late fee, check the date your payment was recorded. If it was within 5 days of the due date, call and ask that the charge be waived.

The late fee can be charged even if it is higher than your minimum payment or even the entire amount that you owe! You can see that if you make a payment of $75, for example, and if $29 goes to late fee and another $20-30 to interest, that paying off the bill will be very slow going.

Use Cards Strategically

One of the biggest advantages of using a credit card is the protection it offers you. Some cards provide a kind of insurance against damaged products and even theft within the first several months of making a purchase. If you have a beef with a merchant and you have paid with a check or cash, you are in a one-down position in bargaining. As soon as the check clears your account, your money is gone. But with a credit card, you can challenge the charge for 60 days, and sometimes longer. So if what you've purchased is defective or if the service is not what was promised, for example, you can challenge the charge. In this case you still have your money and you are in a better bargaining position.

Sometimes it's smart to use a credit card, even though you intend to pay immediately. As soon as the bill comes, you can pay the charge—usually without incurring any interest or other fees. Yet, you still have the power to rescind your payment. An additional benefit is the good record it provides of the transaction—for tax or reimbursement.

Many credit card companies offer frequent-flyer miles. Some business people take advantage of this by charging certain large expenditure on their personal credit cards, then pay it off with their company reimbursement. Then they get the free flier miles, which add up to free trips. This strategy only works if you are very disciplined about quickly paying off the charge, and if your company pays promptly. Otherwise, business charges can add up very fast and you can be in over your head.

Good When You're on the Road

You must have a credit card to rent a car, no matter how much cash you offer as a deposit. The charges are not actually billed until you return the car. If you prefer to pay with cash or a check, you can do so when you settle the bill. Just make sure that the clerk returns all the paper work with your card number on it. And if you pay with cash, make sure you get a receipt—just in case.

If you're on the road a lot, a credit card is handy because you can carry less cash. Plus the bill at the end of the month provides an excellent record for company reimbursement and tax records.

Watch Out for ATMs

On the face of it, paying with an ATM card seems smart. But there are major pitfalls. The ATM looks like a credit card, but it isn't. Instead, it taps right into your savings or checking account. If your ATM card gets into the wrong hands, all the funds in your account can be spent before you know it. You probably have no recourse—especially if the culprit is a relative, like your wayward son. With a credit card you can challenge a relative's charge as "unauthorized." If a credit card is stolen and you report it, your liability is usually limited to fifty dollars.

With an ATM card, you avoid the risk of running up debt, then paying high interest rates and monthly payments, but you take on other dangerous risks. When you or anybody else uses your ATM card, the money is taken out of your account and is gone, without slips to sign or any other paperwork. Not too surprisingly, merchants and banks prefer that you use ATMs, but cash is still accepted.

Pay with Cash

Here's a tip from Suzie Orman, author of *The Courage to Be Rich*. When buying things in your daily life, pay with cash, not your credit card. Always use paper money. Then put all the change you get aside in a jar until the end of the month. If you are like most people, that jar will have $40-60 in it at the end of the month. Transfer this to your savings. Here is money you would have spent without noticing. Try this technique and see how it works for you.

3

Borrow Cautiously

There are many excellent reasons for borrowing money. After deciding to borrow, you have many options regarding how to go about it.

Try Your Bank First

Whenever seeking a loan, always begin with the institution where you do your banking. If you've been there a few years, you've built up a "relationship"—especially if you've made regular deposits at the teller's window. Ask your personal or business banker for advice. This way they get credit for bringing in a loan and you take the inside track to the lending officer. This holds for both home mortgages and credit cards.

Join a Credit Union

Credit unions are co-op banks. Their members pool their savings so that they can lend money to each other. Their loans are better than bank loans, in addition to being easier to get, especially if you have been a member for some time and have a stable job. In many cases you can get a substantial cash advance on your signature alone. Credit unions are usually limited in their membership to certain groups such as to government or company employees or teachers, but there are exceptions. Joining is good insurance against a sudden need for cash, either in a emergency or for some large purchase.

Many credit unions offer "share drafts" which look and work like checks, except that they are written against your savings account, which means your money continues to sit there and earn interest until the draft clears. By comparison, ordinary checking accounts pay little or no interest.

Get An Equity Line Of Credit

If you've owned your home for a few years, you've probably built up *equity*—which is the value of the house above what you still owe. Borrowing against your equity is easy to do. It's called a home equity loan. These loans are both wonderful and potentially very dangerous—even more so than credit cards.

What you get is a line of credit for a particular amount secured by the equity in your home. If you have a lot of equity you can get a credit line of tens of thousands of dollars!

The beauty of it is that, except for a small annual fee, you pay nothing until you draw on your credit line. Then your minimum payment is interest only, at an interest rate considerably less than credit cards but higher than your base mortgage. You are given a checkbook. All you have to do to give yourself a loan is to write a check! You can have a large sum available at your fingertips for a strategic investment, a vacation, your child's college tuition, or an emergency. Yet, it costs nothing until you use it. Federal tax law allows you to deduct the interest you pay on a home equity loan—provided you itemize on Schedule A.

Beware of Debt Consolidation

Because equity interest rates are lower than credit cards, many people transfer debt from credit cards to the equity loan. Doing this with several high balance credit cards is called "debt consolidation." Now you can deduct all the interest on your income tax return. Since the equity loan interest rates are less, your monthly payments go down—initially.

Debt consolidation is fraught with dangers. First off, let's say you consolidate from cards to your equity loan. Before you were making four payments, now you make one. It is easy to pay less and less in that one payment, so that you actually slow down the rate at which you are paying off your debt.

Another danger is that now you have four "clean" credit cards with no balances. It is very easy to run those cards up to the point where they were before. Then you will have doubled the debt you had before consolidation.

At this point many people refinance their home. In the process the equity line is paid off and that debt is moved to your base mortgage and you have only one payment again. After a year or two when the equity has grown, these people get another equity line and repeat the process. Their debt grows and grows and they are on a rat wheel of endless payments.

The greatest danger of consolidating debt onto an equity loan is that you may lose your home.

Get a Margin Account

If you are fortunate enough to have securities and you have very good financial discipline and can handle risk, you can *use* your stocks. Transfer them to a brokerage firm and open a margin account. If you need cash, don't sell your stock—"put them on the margin." What this means is you are taking a loan out on your stock. Once you have the account, you don't have to ask anyone's permission. It's like the equity line of credit on your house but instead of tapping into the equity in your house, you are borrowing on the equity in your stock.

You can borrow just shy of fifty percent of the current value of your stock. Your funds arrive in three to five days. Unlike an equity line of credit on your home, there is no payback demand. Interest is charged on the loan, at a reasonable commercial rate, which is usually about the same as an equity loan—higher than a home mortgage and lower than credit cards—and is *added* to the debt you owe. If you have a hot stock that continues to go up, it may go up enough to cover the amount that you have borrowed. If your hot stock dives, you have just lowered your net worth. When you sell the stock, the brokerage takes back its loan and interest before paying you the balance.

Danger lurks here. If the value of the stock goes down, your *debt stays the same* which means the debt becomes a greater percentage of the value of the stock. The minute that the debt balance goes over fifty per cent of your portfolio's value, you get a "margin call" where your broker calls and tells you how much cash you must send immediately by overnight express to lower your debt to under fifty per cent of the stock's value. In a falling market you can get a margin call every day! If you don't send the money, the brokerage sells enough of your stock to reduce your debt to under fifty percent. This is what happened in the "crash of '29" when there was no fifty percent cap on margin debt. Suddenly, the debt was far greater than the value of the stock and people were jumping out of windows!

You can use this rich person's strategy to fund your education or pay for a heath emergency, for example—if you have good discipline. You don't have to sell your stock. If you think the stock will keep on rising, it is smarter to keep the stock and put it on the margin instead. Make sure you get *good* finanacial advice, however. Don't risk losing stock that is hard to replace on trivial purchases.

Try Friends

Friends with accumulated savings are another possible source of loans. To avoid endangering the friendship, be businesslike: write your arrangement down on paper, including what interest you will pay. Make sure you both have a copy. Set a repayment schedule. If you're borrowing money to put into a business venture, be especially clear—in writing—about the payback terms and if your friend will share in the future profits or get stock options, for example.

Try Pawnbrokers

Pawnbrokers are often used for borrowing money. Basically, you sell low and buy back high! They don't call it selling; they call it a loan. A pawn shop seldom "lends" you more than 15% of the actual value of an object. The item "pawned" is held as collateral. If you can't scrape together the money to redeem your goods by the due date, you lose them. The pawn broker then sells your stuff at market rate and pockets the profit.

Pawning stuff is not the best strategy but if you have valuable things you are not using you can get money for them fast. And your potential losses are limited to the value of the item you pawned.

Avoid Finance Companies

Finance companies, also called "loan sharks" for good reason, are extremely risky. Usually they want the deed to your home as collateral. Be careful because you could lose it. Finance companies advertise widely on TV and target folks with bad credit. The elderly are often taken advantage of by finance companies.

Finance companies routinely charge 16 or more "points," which is a loan fee paid in addition to monthly interest. One point is 1% of the loan value. On a $25,000 loan, you could pay $4000 or more in points (1% = $250 x 16). The points are subtracted from the loan proceeds. So in the example, you would receive $21,000, but repay and pay interest on a loan of $25,000. The actual loan rate is usually the highest amount that can be charged legally. Further, finance companies usually show no mercy if you fall behind. They foreclose and sell your home. Avoid finance companies and use them only as a very last resort.

Don't Co-Sign Friends' Loans

Buyers with weak credit may have to get a "co-signer," especially for large loans for cars or a home. When you co-sign a contract, or "sign a note" as it's sometimes called, you are liable for the entire debt. What you are doing is guaranteeing that your friend or relative will pay, and you promise to pay it if they fail to do so. If this happens you may find yourself in debt for thousands of dollars. Sign notes only for people you'd really be willing and able to pay up for.

Save on Home Mortgages

A standard home mortgage is not the only way to finance the purchase of a house. Look for alternatives.

Look for Private Money

People have been buying and selling houses for thousands of years. It's only been in the latter half of the 20th Century that bank loans became dominant. Many home loans have "points," which is another form of interest called a loan fee. Also, qualifying for traditional loans is filled with hurdles.

If you can't qualify for a bank loan, your answer might be to "get private money." What this means is that the seller loans you the money and there is no bank involved. The deal is between you and the seller. Qualifying can be a casual process, often not much more than a conversation, not like the examination of your navel that goes on with a bank loan, especially if you have had credit problems. Basically all that you have to do is to convince the seller that you are a good risk.

There are no points or fees. Most states have a cap on how much interest a private party can charge—usually 10%. Even though you usually pay a higher interest rate than with a bank loan, your overall costs can be a lot less than with traditional financing. If you were to fall behind in your payments, you have one person to deal with—whom you can probably negotiate with—instead of a cold, mean institution.

Generally, though not always, owners offer to "carry" because they have had some difficulty in selling the property. Maybe it needs work or is in a less desirable neighborhood. That doesn't mean that it is a bad property. It might be just right for you. If you have bad credit, even a bankruptcy, or are young and just getting started, you can still buy a good house if you can find a seller who will carry. In these arrangements, the title company handles all of the paper work and filings. Closing costs are a lot less than with traditional financing, which is another benefit because you usually have to pay for the down payment and the closing costs *both.* The closing costs can add many thousands of dollars to your actual out-of-pocket costs.

Pay Additional Principal

Paying more towards your mortgage than the minimum payment, and specifically designating your additional payment to reduce principal, saves enormous amounts of interest over the years. For example, by paying as little as $25 extra a month, you can save $75,000 or more over a twenty-five year mortgage.

Consider Automatic Withdrawal

Banks love automatic withdrawal payments and will usually reward you for doing it by lowering your interest rate by 1/4%—which can save you thousands of dollars over the life of the loan. All you have to do is to sign an authorization that permits the bank to automatically pay the loan each month from your checking or saving account.

4

Maximize Buying Power

Stretching money is good exercise. The object is *not* simply to pare down your expenses. The trick is to find the areas where doing so will give you a more relaxed, secure, healthy, stylish way of being.

It's easy to spend your life making money until you wake up, at fifty or sixty, and realize that you have only one life to live and that you'd better get on with it, regardless of the economic cost. At this point, many people drop out—undergoing an almost religious conversion, often abandoning lifelong marriages and associations. To their astonishment, they find that they can get along very happily without most of the possessions they formerly strove so hard to buy. They develop new, energy-filled relationships with friends, lovers—even with estranged children. They take risks they would have passed by before, and generally find new excitement and vitality in their lives. But it makes no sense to wait until late in life to discover your own balance between time and money.

Compare Real Costs

If you calculate comparative costs, you can save money—lots of it. Take napkins, for instance. Which is actually cheaper—cloth or paper napkins? You can find out by calculating the average cost in terms of cost per meal or cost per week. Here's how to figure it out. Suppose low-cost paper napkins are 70¢ for a package of 140; this means each napkin costs a half a cent. If you have four people at a table, that comes to 2¢ per meal, 6¢ per day, and 42¢ per week.

Cloth napkins that don't need ironing can be bought for $1, or four for $4. They will need to be laundered about once a week. To figure the average cost, spread the costs out over time. For this example, let's say that cloth napkins will last a year. The cost of washing them is very small because they just go into your general washbasket.

If the cloth napkins last a year and cost $1 each, their average cost per week is about 2¢ each, or 8¢ per week for a family of four. The washing might add 10¢ per week, so the total cloth napkin cost is about 18¢ per week. This is a significant improvement compared to 42¢ per week for paper. Using paper napkins costs three times as much as using cloth napkins. Surprised? This is the power of knowing how to figure cost comparisons.

As a side benefit, using cloth napkins gives you the chance to make your own napkin rings or napkin holders. And it is fun. Clothespins painted different colors work fine, but you can make fancier and more stylish holders. Napkin rings can be carved out of scrap pieces of beautiful hardwood, and metal holders can be etched or enameled with patterns, for example.

Find Hidden Costs

The initial cost of something is only one part of its true cost. Sometimes, as with a light bulb, it's only a fraction of what you will pay to use it; electricity costs far more than the bulb. To assess the real economic impact of a purchase, a full accounting is necessary and includes: *capital loss*—what it costs you to spend your money on that item and not keep it earning interest in the bank; *operating expenses* like the extra electric consumption of a no-frost refrigerator; *repair and maintenance costs*; and finally, *disposal costs*. These costs must all be assessed over the life expectancy of the item, then divided by its lifetime to obtain the yearly cost.

Buy Used

The rapid obsolescence rate is widely bemoaned for its economic and ecological wastefulness. Cars, clothing, and other goods get thrown out long before they wear out. But the fact that things depreciate—lose monetary value—after they're purchased gives canny people a great opportunity for buying things used. A two-year-old used computer, for example, which is better than anything anyone had five years ago, can be gotten for much less than its original price—sometimes free.

Buy Against Trends

Old vinyl records sell for very little compared to CDs, for example. Wherever you can find a strong fashion trend, there's probably an opportunity to go against it and find high-quality things at low prices. If you have a strong personal style and confidence in your own judgment, ignore the current but soon-to-be-outdated fashion and live far "above your means" for very little money.

Barter for Goods and Services

You can barter objects for other objects, but you can also barter services. If you know how to do something—how to quilt or bake bread or do carpentry or wiring—the chances are that you know somebody who needs your knowledge or skill and who can trade some knowledge or skill in return. You can advertise services you want to trade, and what you are looking for, on bulletin boards.

Bartering cements friendships in a way that buying and selling things for cash seldom does. Barterers have to take each other's tastes and personalities into account. They have to deal with each other as human beings. One of the reasons to grow vegetables, or keep bees, or raise chickens, is that you'll have surpluses to use in bartering. That is half the fun.

Avoid Mail-Order and TV Sales

The art of deceptive catalog descriptions has reached remarkable heights. Too often, merchandise turns out to be junky and twice the cost of what you'd pay in a store, once shipping costs are included. Colors can be different from the pictures. Sizes are unpredictable. What you get for paying about double store prices is the chance to look over merchandise and return it at your own expense—if it isn't really what you expected. The only things safe to buy "sight unseen" are standardized items like books, music recordings, and software where you know exactly what you are buying.

Use Coupons Wisely

The "29¢ off" type of coupon can persuade you to purchase something you hadn't planned to purchase. When the coupon is for something you are planning on buying then it's wise to use the coupon. Considering the costs of operating a car, however, it's almost never worth it to make a special trip to some store just to cash in on a coupon or two. Also, be careful not to buy a more expensive "brand name" product just because you have a coupon for it. On the other hand, a coupon may provide an economical way to test a different brand.

Scavenge for Free Stuff

Households and industries throw out an astounding quantity of perfectly usable pans, paper, clothes, appliances, boards, springs, tools, metal, cloth, and glass. People throw out valuable motors, fishing equipment, tires, garden equipment, and chairs whose only fault may be something as simple as a missing rung that you can replace in minutes with a dowel. Some of the most interesting objects are discarded merely because they're old. Frequently, these objects are of a better quality than new ones.

Be Creative

The extent to which you can make use of "waste" material is limited only by your own ingenuity. Given enough of it, you could construct a whole house and furnish it comfortably and cozily without spending any money at all—in theory anyway. There's a whole school of interior decoration known as "junk chic." Against plain white walls, brightly painted discarded items can look fantastic. Weird finds from flea markets and junk shops give character to a room.

The key is to learn to look at things without preconceptions. Maybe that funny-looking metal bracket would make a clothes rack. That nice broad piece of wood could look good as a shelf. And isn't it possible that that abandoned pair of wheels would be fine for a garden cart or a kid's pushcart?

Stock Up on Bargains

It's often wise to buy standard necessities in bulk and ask for quantity or casc discounts; besides, it saves gas and tedious trips to the store. Many people do this for toilet paper, soap, shampoo, canned or frozen foods they use regularly, rice, lentils, and other staples, cleaning materials, light bulbs, and especially pet food. Dog and cat food can be purchased by the case or large bag in warehouse stores like CostCo for 50%, or even less, than in pet stores.

But, of course, there's a limit—usually the size of your storage space. Only stock up on things that don't spoil, rot, or mildew under your storage conditions. Don't overestimate your consumption rate. Preserved foods lose much of their nutritive value if kept more than six months or so. Inventory your house and jot down the things to keep an eye out for at discounts: coffee, toothpaste, paper supplies, and durable goods like towels and sheets.

5

Be a Savvy Shopper

If you want to develop and maintain your own style, these rules of thumb will come in handy. Remember that shopping is a game of wits!

Be Skeptical of Brand Names

Advertisements brainwash the unsuspecting into thinking that brand names hold a kind of magic. Is one brand of aspirin superior to other aspirin, when all aspirin is chemically identical? The greatest differences among products lie in packaging, which means that buyers who simply buy brand names are not necessarily getting better quality in the goods.

Since differences from one brand to another are small, a lot of money has to be spent to convince you to buy a particular brand. Advertisers try to make you feel that by purchasing their product you will be sexier, wiser, handsomer, cleaner, or less worried. But if you have confidence in yourself and your own style of living, you don't need to rely on the fantasy that a product can really change who you are.

For expensive purchases, research which brand is best. Your library has a collection of *Consumer Reports* back issues, with elaborate quality tests and information on safety hazards, breakdown rates, and so forth. Spending a few hours browsing *Consumer Reports* once in a while will save you both money and confusion.

Beware of Deceptive Packaging

Companies are absolutely shameless in their attempts to bamboozle you—and most of the time they get away with it. The bottle for one big-name shampoo bottle, for instance, used to be simple and round and contained sixteen ounces—an even pint. They switched to new bottles that were taller, thinner, shaped funny, and held only fifteen ounces—but the price went up! So don't assume that a taller bottle holds more than a shorter bottle. Check the quantity printed on the package or the "unit price"—cost per ounce—that by law must be posted on the shelf.

Packaging is not only deceptive, but also ecologically destructive and wasteful. Sometimes the fancy printing, special shapes, and plastic wrappers actually cost more than the product. When the prices are similar, you're better off buying things in simple packages.

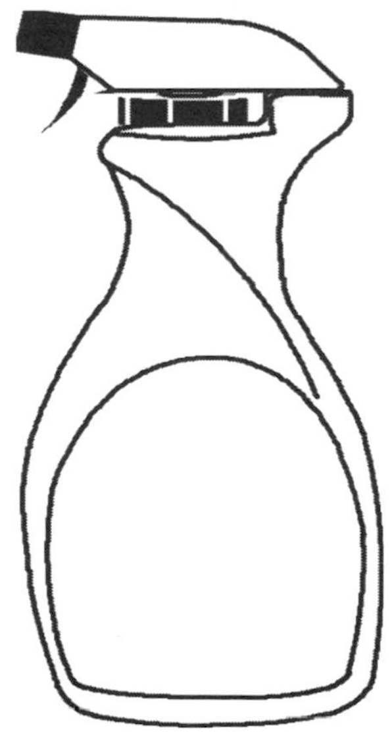

Even simple packages can be deceptive. For example, carrots are packed in plastic which has thin orange stripes printed on it to make the carrots look more orange. Similarly, grocery stores sometimes use pink lights to make meat look redder. You can buy many foods "in bulk," with no packaging at all—this reduces the price and the ecological destruction of your purchase.

Watch for Deceptive Pricing

"List" or "original" prices are often not real prices, but fictitious prices set somewhat higher than what the seller really wants to get. Then when they offer a "discount," you may think you've gotten a bargain.

Check the Contents

Beware of items that have labels reading "15¢ off regular price!" or something like that. Such labels are often deceiving. Check the quantity in the package compared to other brands—the contents may have been cut down.

Do Comparisons

Fairly standard prices can be found in the Sears mail-order catalog. If some store is offering "bargain" towels but you see good towels in the catalog for less than half the "bargain" price, it is obviously not a good deal. To get a Sears mail-order catalog of your own, you usually have to be a regular customer—but you can always look at it in Sears stores, and in some libraries. There's practically nothing, except cars, that the Sears catalog doesn't offer.

Be Sure it's a Different Product

Be on guard against "refinements" to a product that are used to justify higher prices. To add fragrance and coloring to a detergent may not increase its manufacturing cost at all, but its retail price is usually higher than if the detergent were unadorned. Soap with a fancy label and a special smell doesn't wash you any cleaner than a soap without these "features." In many "boutique" stores, practically all the merchandise is of the fancy, inflated-price variety.

6

Rework Buying Habits

Don't limit your shopping to malls, with their all-too-familiar offerings. It's fun to try alternative sources, where merchandise is more varied and unusual than in the big chain outlets.

Buy at Auctions

Auctions can be a good source for furniture, rugs, clothes, books, and many other things—if you can resist crowd psychology. But if you're easily stampeded, you can find yourself paying more for something at an auction than it costs new. Go to the preview beforehand, look at the goods. Then check a Sears catalog to make sure you know what a fair price is. Bid only on things you want, and set a top limit beforehand. Control yourself by bringing only so much cash so you can't overbid. Most auction houses accept cash only.

Entertain Yourself

Auctions can be a form of no-cost entertainment—they can be fun even when you buy nothing. Dedicated auction-goers enjoy the feel of the bidding: When is it petering out? When will it go hopelessly higher? When is the bidding by a determined professional who has a rich customer lined up? When is it a piece of junk that nobody wants? When is someone bidding against you to push the price up? Auctions are particularly fun for those who like to match wits with others in games like chess and checkers.

Use Bulletin Boards

One of the great social inventions is the *community bulletin board,* on which people post notices of things they want to sell or buy or do. Bulletin boards are commonly found around colleges, in laundromats, in supermarkets, nailed up outside stores, on houses, and increasingly on the Internet. If none exists in your neighborhood, start one—pick a busy, heavy foot-traffic location, and ask a storekeeper if you can nail up a big board somewhere. Seed it with a few cards from your friends and see what happens. A careful buyer can always do better by buying direct from a previous owner than from a dealer.

Shop at Discount Warehouses

Discount stores and buying clubs exist in most cities. They sell merchandise of all kinds at prices noticeably lower than the prices in regular stores. Their membership requirements mean paying for a card, but most people save that amount on their first visit.

Be cautious, however, because some discounters sell inferior brands that look like more expensive ones but lack certain features. If you buy a refrigerator because the discounter is selling it for less than an appliance store or Sears, you may discover later that it isn't as good as other machines. Check model numbers and descriptions carefully. Also, because discounters and clubs are big-volume operators, they aren't generally interested in honoring guarantees and usually don't have service departments.

Frequent Second-Hand Shops

The Salvation Army and other helpful organizations maintain thrift stores where, if you have an eye for quality, you can pick up clothes and household items for a small fraction of new prices. Consignment stores, which take in goods from people wanting to sell them, sometimes offer high-quality or even luxury items very cheaply. And you may be able to sell some of what you are not using to pick up a little extra cash.

Buy at Garage Sales

You get the best deals in garage sales, especially when somebody is moving and anxious to get rid of stuff. You have to develop a quick, ruthless eye to avoid spending too much time on any individual collection of junk. It helps to have a half-formed shopping list in your mind for such occasions. The main joy, of course, is in finding things you didn't remember you wanted until you saw them. And then there's also the joy of haggling, which most people seem to expect.

Flea market-type classified papers are used to announce garage and yard sales. Sometimes people put up notices on telephone poles on the day of their sale. Beware of "permanent" garage sales, which are really secondhand shops with correspondingly higher prices.

Flea markets are generally worth the trouble only if they're held by some organization on an occasional basis. Regularly established ones are mainly filled with secondhand dealers selling tired collections of battered tools, old radios, overpriced antique jewelry, and well-worn kitchen implements. Some of them even act as an outlet for stolen clothes, cameras, and electronic stuff.

Buy from Recyclers

Clever entrepreneurs have discovered that there's gold in what used to be waste. They buy and sell used windows, doors, lumber, hardware, tools, electric devices, glass, and so on. They also sometimes make deals with cities to scavenge stuff from the refuse station or dump. If you need to fix something, check with a salvager.

7

Plan Before Shopping

With a little planning, you can eat tasty, interesting, and high-quality food cheaply. Always eat before grocery shopping because if you are hungry when shopping you'll tend to buy more. Make a shopping list of what you intend to buy and stick to it. Otherwise, it's easy to get to browsing over what you might buy and next thing you know your basket is filled with stuff you didn't intend to buy. Buy for a whole week—or even two weeks. The less often you go into a store, the less you will spend. Impulse shopping can get very expensive.

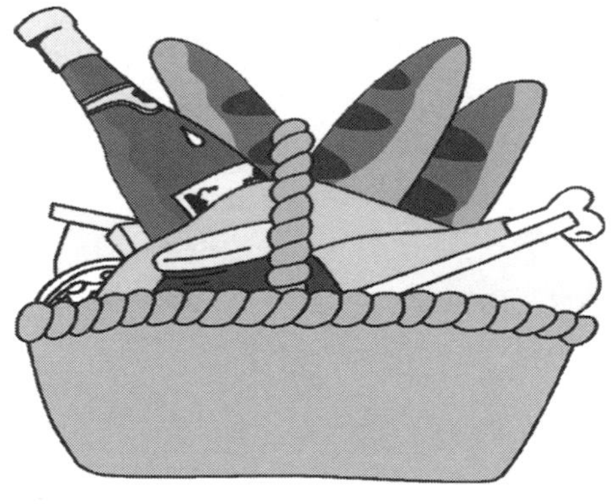

Buy Food in Grocery Stores

Food in grocery stores is usually half as expensive as prepared food—and it's usually better quality with less unhealthy salt, sugar, and fat. If you're longing to try a particular restaurant, try it for lunch—not dinner—because you'll get the same food at a lower price. Carry an apple or a bunch of crackers in your pocket, purse, or backpack for snacks between meals.

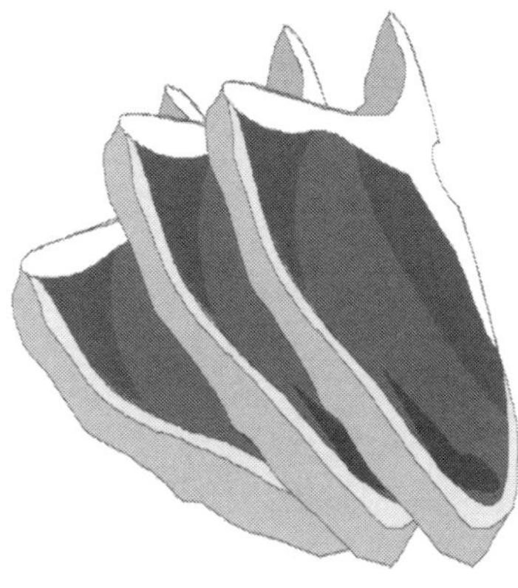

Buy Cheaper Grades of Meat

The cheaper grades, "Good" instead of "Choice," are nourishing and tasty. Certain cuts like chuck roasts and chuck steaks, for example, are less expensive, yet still tender. Rolled roasts have less waste than rib roasts—so you actually get more for your money.

Eat Organ Meats

Kidney, liver, heart, and brain may seem "icky" but they can be delicious and they're cheap. Beef heart, cut into quarter-inch slices, can be fried in a few minutes, and tastes delicious in any kind of tomato-and-onion sauce. Brain, which is a high-protein food, is delicious with scrambled eggs. It is also high in cholesterol, however, and should be eaten only once or twice a month. The same goes for liver which often contains high levels of toxins from the feed the animals eat.

Make Dog and Cat Treats

Organ meats are wonderful for making dog and cat treats. Your pets will love you for it. Boil the organ meat until it is well cooked. Then slice it into strips and lay out on a cookie tray. Put into your oven on very low heat until it is completely dry.

Eat More Poultry

Lean ground turkey is a better buy than hamburger, which has a lot of fat. Chicken, turkey, duck, and goose are excellent and relatively inexpensive protein sources. Avoid pre-stuffed frozen poultry, which costs more and the stuffing is a food-poisoning hazard. Certain chicken parts are very cheap, like backs, which are fine for soups, and chicken livers, which are a wonderful delicacy when fried.

One idea is to roast a whole chicken in your oven. If it is a large one, it will be almost like a Thanksgiving turkey with crispy skin. After feasting to your delight, pop all the bones and left overs into a large pot filled with water and let it boil for a few hours. Then remove the bones and add vegetables and spices and you have a wonderful soup for almost nothing.

Buy Vegetables Fresh

Buy vegetables in season when they are cheap and good. Don't go too much by appearance; sometimes the biggest, shiniest fruit is also the blandest and mealiest. Most fruit is picked early so that it can be shipped to market before ripening. Your best buy is a day or two's supply of fruit that's on the verge of being perfectly ripe.

Frozen vegetables, paradoxically, are often actually fresher because they're picked, washed, and frozen right in the fields which makes them more tasty and nutritious than fresh ones that have been traveling and in storage for a few days. Frozen vegetables are usually cheaper than their fresh counterparts, especially off-season. Peas, green beans, and corn are even cheaper when you buy them in bulk bags rather than the small square cardboard packages.

Buy "off" Brands

Supermarket chains and other large marketers sell "house brands" of foods, drugs, and other goods under their own labels. Because they're generally unadvertised, they are cheaper. In canned goods, buy Grade B; it's as tasty as Grade A, just not as perfect in appearance. You pay a lot extra to get all-perfect fruits, especially. If you can find cans labeled "broken pieces"—of peaches, pears, and so on—they're cheaper still, but just as tasty and nutritious.

Buy Perishables in Small Quantities

Be careful in buying perishables; the most expensive food is one that goes bad before it can be eaten. Buy only what you will use right away when the item is perishable. Bundles of vegetables can be redone: unwind the wires and take only what you need from an asparagus bundle, for example. Or have the butcher repackage a few steaks. There is no need to buy more perishables than you need.

Buy Direct from Farmers

Farmers markets offer produce straight from the farm and at prices lower than in stores. And it's a lot of fun. Many farmers who sell at such markets grow organically, without chemical fertilizers or pesticides. If you have a predictable need for vegetables and fruits, consider joining a Community Supported Agriculture Cooperative—which you can find on bulletin boards—where you agree to buy X dollars worth of seasonal fresh food every week from a nearby farm. It's delivered to your door without being transported thousands of miles like most supermarket stuff. You become, in effect, a stockholder in the farm—often, you and your kids can visit the source of your food and sometimes even help out, which is highly educational for all of you.

Buy Staples in Bulk

Avoid buying packaged sliced meats and cheese because slicing and slick packaging can more than double the price per pound. Many grains, nuts, dried fruits, and other foods are available in bulk—cheaper than their packaged counterparts.

Food that is pre-packaged or pre-measured costs even more in small quantities which means you pay more for small boxes of tea bags, for cereal in individual-portion boxes, for potato chips in small bags, and so forth. Buying prepackaged vegetables not only costs more but also exposes you to the preservatives used to keep the contents fresh-looking.

Buy Dried Milk

The protein, or body-building power, of nonfat dried milk is equal to that of whole milk with the health advantage of having no fat and being much cheaper, more compact to store, and spoil resistant. Keep the powder packages, tightly closed, in a cool cupboard.

Really Chill It

Dried milk, once mixed, improves with age for a day or so; mix as much up at once as you can. For best taste, dried milk must be especially cold when you drink it. Mix your supply of milk in advance of when you'll drink it so that it has time for the refrigerator to cool it down. If you mix it after supper, for example, the next day's supply is ready in the morning.

8

Cheap Classy Drinks

Soft drinks have little food value. They are fattening, tooth rotting, and very expensive. Candy is mostly sugar—calories without much nutritive value. Many so-called fruit juices contain only tiny percentages of fruit juice, as a review of their labels reveals. The main ingredients are water, sugar, corn syrup, and mysterious chemical "flavorings."

Drink Tea

Tea is one of the least expensive drinks, aside from plain water. It is cheapest when you buy it loose by the pound. A pound makes well over two hundred cups of tea. Most tea bags contain enough tea for two cups, so you waste tea if you use a new bag for each cup; use the bag for a second cup or save it for later.

The handiest way to brew just one or two cups of loose tea is with a perforated spoon-with-a-lid that you can buy in housewares stores. Tea should brew for three to five minutes. Don't judge strength by color—some leaves have more coloring in them.

Wonderful Varieties

There are three types of tea. Most common in America is *black tea,* which has a smooth flavor and bright color. *Oolong tea* is partly brownish and partly greenish; it has not been fermented as much as black tea and makes a lighter-colored tea. *Green tea,* which is widely drunk by Asian peoples, is not fermented at all, and gives a very light, sometimes almost colorless tea.

The real fun of tea is in experimenting with different types and finding those you really prefer. To do this you have to locate a store specializing in teas. Such stores are usually delightfully aromatic and friendly places. Some have bars where you can taste the different types before you buy. These teas have lovely names: Lapsang Souchong, Gunpowder, Jasmine, Keemun, Uva.

There are many interesting mint and herbal teas that do not contain thein or tannin which makes them easier on your system. Some of them, like ginseng, are believed to have energizing properties. Fruit teas are a wonderful treat, in addition to being inexpensive. Commercially sweetened iced tea drinks are actually an expensive combination of artificial flavor, sugar, and a little tea powder. A healthier, tastier—and yes, cheaper—way to fix up iced tea is to add a little orange juice to a batch of black tea and chill it.

Drink Stylish Coffee Cheaply

Most shops selling fine roasted coffee beans will sell partial pound quantities so you can buy just a little to try out different roasts. You can often get a free cup to taste in the store, too.

Look in thrift shops and at garage sales for a second hand one-cup espresso maker called a *macchinetta*, which is that little silver pot that you fill, heat, then turn upside down. Clean out old deposits by filling it with boiling water and a little baking soda.

Instant coffee costs about half as much per cup as freeze-dried coffee. Its advantage, besides cost, is that it requires only a cup and a spoon to make. Designer instant coffees, with or without a shot of brandy, and a glob of whipped cream on top, make a fancy offering for guests.

Try Instant Drinks

Packaged hot chocolate mix, if made with milk, gives a protein pick-up and comes in exotic flavors. There are also instant apple cider drinks, which are quite good for wintery special occasions.

9

Save on Household Goods

Even low-quality houseware is quite expensive when bought new. This is particularly true in the kitchen. When stocking a kitchen, thrift stores can be immensely helpful. As with everything else, an open mind and some creativity come in handy too.

Buy Inexpensive Dishes

Eating is one of the most personal, intimate things you do, so don't corrupt it by eating from things that have a bad look, feel, or smell. Dishes need not be all alike. A table will, in fact, be more intriguing if every place is set differently. Secondhand stores are loaded with dishes of all kinds—many genuine china. Look for good individual items that really interest you. If they genuinely hit you, you'll almost always find that they also go together nicely—they may be different sizes or weights but they'll have a common spirit. There's nothing wrong with a chip or two. A beautiful old plate is still a beautiful old plate, even if it's nicked.

People with small children may want to consider "unbreakable" dishes that are actually a kind of glass that won't break or chip if dropped on a wooden floor. They have a slightly glassy surface, but they do come in plain, reasonably attractive colors.

Buy Stainless-Steel Utensils

Stainless steel flatware doesn't wear through or peel the way silver plate does. Secondhand stores usually have big boxes full of assorted cast-off knives, forks, and spoons. Learn to spot used stainless by its soft gray color and its hard feel. Silver plate tends to be a bit yellowed, and often you can see brass or rusty steel peeking out. Pick items that have plain lines and a good heft to them. New stainless steel in pleasant, and sometimes elegant, designs can be bought fairly cheaply in import outlets and houseware super stores.

Find Practical Knives

Don't settle for a knife that doesn't look and feel right to you. The manner in which the handle is fixed to the blade needs special attention. Is it firm enough to take stress? If there is metal binding around the handle ends, is it flimsy? If there is no hilt, is there a rounded, projecting heel on the blade so that your hand can't slip onto the blade? Are there places where cracks may open up to catch food particles and harbor bacteria? Does the brass or bronze or other metal of the handle go well with the color of the blade?

Price isn't a reliable indication of the quality of a knife. You can pay a great deal of money for a practically useless stainless-steel knife. On the other hand, no really good knife is cheap. But you can get a carbon-steel knife that will last you for decades for a reasonable price. If you look carefully in second hand stores you can usually pick up a good knife for very little money.

Sharpen Your Knives

A knife made of good carbon steel can be re-sharpened for years and will retain a keen edge. Carbon steel can discolor from food acids like tomato juice, and it will rust if left wet. But this doesn't hurt its cutting ability, and you may like the irregular dark patina that develops. You also can keep it burnished with metal polish or steel wool. Frequent sharpening keeps knives in good health and can be an aesthetic experience.

Don't use wall sharpeners or other grinder-type sharpeners because you may grind away your blade and never get it sharp. It's better to get a sharpening steel. Or you can use a small stone—they're cheap and come on wooden handles, which makes them convenient to hold in the hand so you can strop the blade on them. Buy one in a specialized knife store and ask for a demonstration.

Buy Inexpensive Pots and Pans

Secondhand stores have a good supply of heavy old frying pans and pots of many sizes. In general, the heavier a pan is, the better, because it will conduct heat more evenly. Stainless-steel-lined pots are the easiest to keep clean, the most durable and healthy to use. The best contain copper or aluminum bottoms, which aid heat distribution. Get pots with tight-fitting lids because they save a lot of heat and help in cooking vegetables quickly. It may be worth it to buy a brand-new lid to go with a cheap secondhand pot, even though you spend more on the lid. Avoid aluminum which believed to be a cause of Alzheimer's Disease.

Get Good Mirrors Cheaply

Every house needs a full-length mirror—people like them and it is important for a baby to see its entire body. New mirrors are expensive, but secondhand stores sell mirrors at reasonable prices, especially when they have a cracked corner or a little patch of the silver backing missing. Check that the mirror is really flat—stand back at least ten feet from it and see if it gives a true reflection. A wavy mirror is madness-making. If you find a good flat mirror with small defects or an ugly frame, you can always take the frame off or paint it.

Take a Cloth Bag Shopping

Cloth bags have been gaining popularity for use as shopping bags. They can fulfill many purposes other than saving a few cents at the grocery store. The fact that these bags collapse to almost nothing means that everyone in your household can carry one with them.

Buy Cheap Clocks

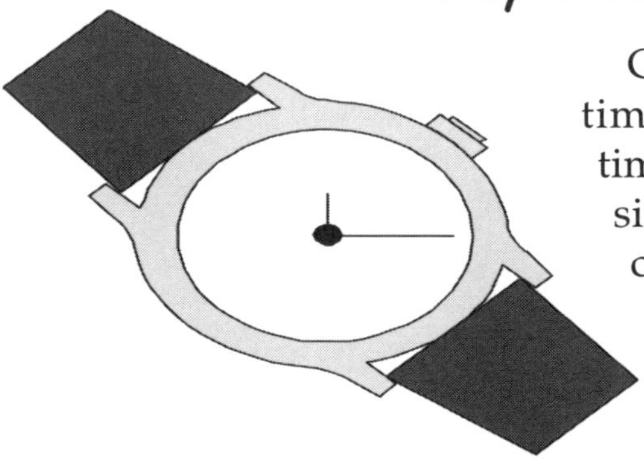

Cheap mass-produced timepieces keep better time than many expensive jeweled heirloom clocks. You can probably find a type you can treasure—for a while. Buy cheap watches and throw them away. Usually they'll keep time for five years or so. The same is true for alarm clocks. Solar-cell powered wrist watches never need batteries—they were the first real mass-market application of solar power.

The watch, like the time clock and the business suit, is usually a symbol of servitude. Try "losing" your watch once in a while. You'll probably find that you get through the day just as well without it—and it might be relaxing.

10

Buy Fewer Appliances

A key to a stylish life is to own *only* those things that you need or want, and *not* clutter your life—and space. If you don't waste money on buying and maintaining things of little use to you, then you'll have more money and more time to spend on what you truly value. If your head is obsessed with things, you can't pay attention to living with style—how you think, how you express yourself in words, clothes, projects, your ways of doing stuff.

So let's look at the kinds of things that people have in their homes, whether you really need them, and how to get the best use out of them.

Minimize Appliances

People trying to live cheaply with simple style, minimize dependence on appliances as well as their energy consumption. What's a reasonable minimum? In my experience: refrigerator, stove, stereo, blender, toaster, and iron. A computer and video player makes sense, too.

Over a five-year lifetime, you'll spend more than the purchase price of an appliance on energy to run it. Frost-free refrigerators, upright freezers, and air conditioners are particularly heavy energy users. Since most appliances are constructed to last at least ten years—refrigerators and freezers up to twenty—on the whole you'll get better value for your money if you buy secondhand.

Avoid Service Agreements

If you buy something new, you'll be asked to buy an "extended warranty" or "service agreement." Careful research by *Consumer Reports* indicates that generally they are not a good value. Most lemons reveal themselves pretty quickly—while the appliance is still under the manufacturer's warranty—often in the first few days or weeks while the warranty is still in effect. Service agreements are deceptively expensive—especially since you usually never use the service. Often as much as 15% is added to the purchase price. If you finance the purchase, you pay interest on the warranty, which further increases its cost in a hidden way. If the appliance does break down, it is almost always cheaper to pay for a simple service call at the time, than to have paid for a service agreement for months or years.

Don't Use an Air Conditioner

Air conditioners were virtually unknown at the end of World War II. Now they are one of our greatest consumers of household energy. People have become so convinced they cannot live without air conditioners that they keep their dwelling windows closed, with their conditioner running full blast, even when they would get cooler faster by opening a couple of windows.

Money spent on insulation will quickly be repaid in lower air-conditioner operating costs—or in not having to rely on one at all. If you feel you *have* to have one and are good with electricity, here's a neat trick. Wire a simple outdoor thermosensor, a dial set at the temperature you're asking your air conditioner to achieve, and a bell. When the outdoor temperature is lower than the temperature you're after indoors, the bell rings. In one experiment, households with such devices cut electricity consumption by 16%.

Minimize Small Appliances

You can do everything an electric frying pan will do in a heavy iron skillet. You can do everything a toaster oven or microwave oven will do in your stove.

Use a Food Processor

A food processor will chop up and purée practically any kind of fruit or vegetable. So you can produce mixtures as cool as those offered by a juice bar: celery and cabbage juice, plum and apple juice, apricot and pineapple juice. You can also make cheap baby food, puréed broccoli soup, carrot cake, zucchini bread, walnut butter, and sauces to pour over ice cream.

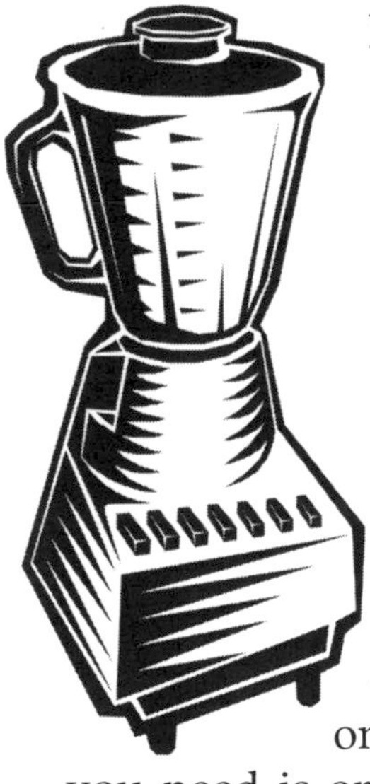

Blenders are a cheap alternative to food processors. They are simple machines that either work or don't, so look for a secondhand one. Try it. If it works, buy it. All you need is one whose motor runs, whose top stays on, and whose bottom isn't cracked. Make sure to test it with water in it before buying.

Buy a Simple Toaster

If you're buying a toaster secondhand, make sure it works. The handle should stay down, then pop up briskly. All the heating element wires—the flat wires inside that turn red—should heat up on both sides of each piece of bread. Check the cord and if it is worn or frayed don't buy the toaster. See if the adjustment for darker or lighter toast works. The bottom should open so you can clean out crumbs that collect.

Some recent toasters don't have a push-down handle; you put the bread in the slot and the toaster lowers it automatically. This fancy feature, like most extras, is likely to require expensive repairs. The same goes for "humidity-control" features. A toaster is a simple machine designed to do only one thing, reliably. Get a simple one.

Toasters are not always worth repairing, since the repairs may cost more than a new toaster. If you're good at repairing, however, or have a handy friend, it's worth opening up the toaster to see what's wrong.

Buy a Used Vacuum Cleaner

If you have rugs or carpets, a heavy upright vacuum with rotating brush will beat out most of the dust. There's not much that can go wrong with a vacuum. You're likely to get a good deal on a secondhand one. Let it run a while when you try it out and make sure it really picks up dust. Try it on a little sand—that takes good suction. Holding your hand over the hose isn't a good test. Don't be impressed by attachments.

Save on a Refrigerator

A refrigerator less than five years old can be expected to give many years of service, and many older machines still have plenty of life in them. But make sure you turn on a secondhand refrigerator for a while before buying it to see if it also freezes ice. Listen to the motor to see if it labors, especially when starting up. Equally important is making sure that it turns off and doesn't run constantly, which consumes electricity and costs a fortune.

You can save money by keeping the refrigerator set to 40°F. Measure the temperature with an ordinary household thermometer in the middle of the box for ten to fifteen minutes. Putting it at the warmest setting will usually suffice. Don't make the mistake of putting it at the coldest setting. Not only will you waste power and money, you may freeze your vegetables, which is like throwing money away. If it has a separate temperature control for the freezer, set it to 0°F.

Check the door gasket and install a new one if it is loose. Check the gasket's tightness by putting a sheet of paper against it and shutting the door; if the paper slips out, the gasket is probably shot.

Make sure your refrigerator is no bigger than you really need. A big box wastes more energy than a small one; it may also waste food that gets hidden. Apartment-size boxes have come on the market—counter-high so you can prepare food on top, with a freezer compartment for temporarily keeping frozen foods.

Avoid Frost-Free Models

Frost-free models cost up to 100% more to run, besides costing more to buy. They also have complex circuitry, fans, and heaters that break down. Defrosting a refrigerator merely requires turning a switch and removing the water as the ice melts.

Don't Own a Washer and Dryer

Washers and dryers are expensive appliances and when breakdowns occur they can cost half of what a new machine does. Unless you have a great deal of washing to do, you may be better off to use the laundromat—or to share a washer and dryer with a couple of neighbors. These machines are not harmed by being outdoors unless it gets so cold that water can freeze in the hoses or piping, so in mild climates they can stand on a covered back porch or in a shed.

Small loads are wasteful of water and energy. If you have a washer with an adjustment for load size, don't forget to use it. Incidentally, the clothesline is making something of a comeback—solar-powered drying! Sun drying disinfects diapers. It is also cheap and gives all your clothes a distinctive, wonderful smell.

Buy a "Trailing Edge" Computer

Computers are extremely useful for gathering information and communicating with friends and family via the Internet. It doesn't make sense to buy an expensive computer new—unless you use it for work. The technology upgrades very fast. Three-year-old machines often sell for 20% of their original price. Buy on the "trailing edge" and get fantastic cyber-capabilities for very little money. Then upgrade to a new "old" system every few years to cheaply keep up.

11

Gather Food

Being self-reliant about some of what you eat won't take you back to pioneer days, but it will give you the important satisfaction of knowing just what you're eating and where it came from. It fosters a delightful feeling of independence from "the system."

Gather Edible Wild Plants

Foraging for wild plants is a hobby that can provide you with a great deal of tasty food. Wild plants abound in cities as well as the country. Wash them carefully, especially if they grow near streets or roads. It's useful wisdom to know which plants growing in your region are edible. Here are some of the most common.

Dandelions

This so called "weed" is full of vitamins and can be eaten in salads or boiled like spinach. The small new leaves are the tenderest. In the spring, dandelion roots can be sliced and boiled. Roots can also be dried, ground up, and brewed to make a tasty tea. Chicory roots, similarly, are dried, ground, and added to New Orleans-style coffee.

Mustard

This wild plant is also grown commercially. It is good boiled when young. Use the big leaves, not top ones, and simmer 30 minutes.

Acorns

A nutritious staple of Native Americans, acorns *must* be leached to be edible. This is done by boiling them whole for two hours, then running large quantities of water over them, or by rinsing them with several changes of water.

You can eat acorns as a meal or mush. You can even candy them. To make a flour that will keep for a while, grind up the fresh acorns, leach by mixing with boiling water, and press out through a cloth. Repeat this several times, then spread thinly in a pan and place in the oven or in hot sunlight to dry.

Berries

Blackberries are widely available. Blueberries grow wild in many areas; so do huckleberries, strawberries and cherries. As in eating any wild plants, study identification guidebooks with an expert outdoors person before eating anything because some berries are poisonous.

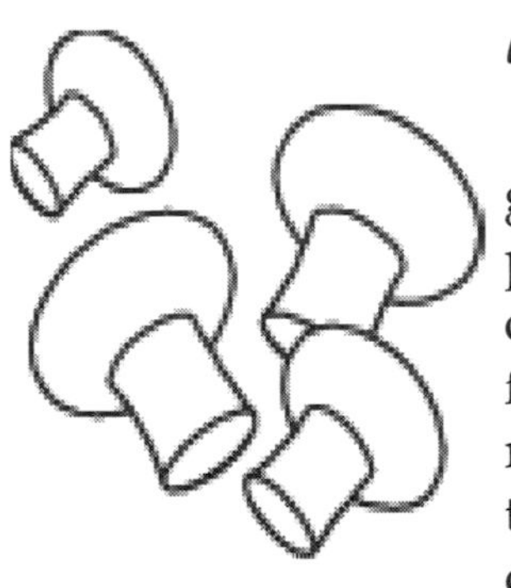

Mushrooms

With a good identification guidebook and an experienced person to alert you to the dangerous types, you can have a lot of fun gathering mushrooms. Some mushrooms are absolutely delectable, and mushroom hunting is one of the nicest ways to spend an otherwise dreary wet day.

Nuts

Walnuts, hickory nuts, and hazelnuts are tasty and good sources of protein for the diet. Sunflower seeds, which grow wild in some areas, are loaded with nutrition.

Greens

Watercress grows wild by many springs; it's related to nasturtiums, whose leaves are a delicacy in salads. Wild onions can flavor your dishes. Clover blossoms and mint leaves make good tea. Dry them away from heat or sunlight. Catnip tea is reputed to be a good sedative.

12

Make Food

There is a joy in making your own food from scratch. It's fun and you can save a bundle.

Bake Bread

Home-baked bread is amazingly inexpensive and you avoid the additives and preservatives found in most commercial breads. It is easy to make bread. It just takes mixing, kneading, and patience—you have to wait for it to "rise." The smell of baking bread is wonderfully homey, too. If you get into baking a lot of bread, you might want to check out a warehouse club or discount store for a bread-making machine. These machines do the mixing and kneading for you. They can produce a wide range of bread: from the healthiest whole-wheat, to a fairly crusty "French" white loaf, to raisin and other fruit breads.

Once you get into the basic routine of baking, you'll probably branch out into all kinds of delectable and cheap pastries, cakes, pies, rolls, and muffins. Don't be confined to a supermarket for flours. Health-foods stores usually have a range of grain flours to choose from. Tasty homemade bread seldom remains uneaten very long, but you can store it in the freezer or refrigerator if needed.

Drink Inexpensive Alcohol

Drink standard-brand American wine, unless you live in a wine-making region where you can find good stuff even cheaper. In small quantities, wine can actually benefit your heart. It relaxes you and provides some vitamins, as well as calories of food energy. Wine can make the difference between just a meal and an elegant repast.

Make Beer and Wine

It's legal to make your own wine and beer. Because of spoilage, wastage, and other factors, however, home winemaking can't reliably produce wine at a significantly lower price than gallon jugs of commercial wine. Home brewing beer is much easier and costs about 20% as much as commercial beer.

Home brew contains more alcohol, has more vitamins since it isn't heavily filtered, and has a richer taste than commercial beers. You can make draft beer, which is flat, or fizzy beer, which can have more carbonization than commercial. Specialized stores sell beer-making supplies and provide the simple directions.

Make Yogurt

Yogurt is easy to make and it's a delicious and healthy dessert or snack, especially when a little fruit or jam is added. Buttermilk and kefir are two other cultured milk drinks you might try making. Basic cookbooks such as *The Joy of Cooking* give easy-to-follow procedures for making yogurt. An expensive yogurt-making rig is not necessary; it's easy to improvise what you need.

13

Grow Food

Growing your own food can save you money while assuring you that no pesticide residues are on what you eat. Perhaps even more important, growing productive plants as part of your life connects you to the underlying biological realities of the planet. It teaches you and your children about nurturing other living things, which in turn nurture us. When you think of it, it is living with style. Once you get some experience in gardening, you may even feel like branching out to keeping bees and raising chickens or fish.

Grow Vegetables

City people as well as those in suburbs or small towns are turning increasingly to gardening as a source of wholesome, inexpensive food and pleasant recreation. Many city dwellings have backyards, balconies, or roofs where food can be grown either in the ground or in planter boxes, barrels, recycled bathtubs, etc.

Find Free Materials

You can probably borrow or get for free a spade, rake, hoe, and watering hose. You can probably find scrap lumber to use for constructing planter boxes. A vacant lot can provide a source of soil. Your local sewage plant probably has free fertilizer sludge, usable on all but root vegetables. Dig it in during the fall. You may also be able to find free mulch material, which greatly decreases watering and weeding. Better yet, make your own from lawn clippings, rice hulls, even newspapers cut into thin strips.

Get Good Advice

Good gardening books abound. Look in your library. Talk to experienced gardeners to find out what kinds of vegetables thrive best in your locale and soil type and which are prone to diseases and insects. Limit your first growing experiments to local favorites.

Great advances have been made in productivity on small plots, using techniques of deep digging, raised beds, and close planting to keep down soil temperatures and conserve moisture. Look for information about BioDynamic or French Intensive methods.

Start with Easy to Grow Vegies

Some plants, like zucchini and other squash, are virtually fail proof and produce unbelievable yields. Most people have success with tomatoes, peas, beans, carrots, lettuce, and corn. All these foods taste immensely better fresh and are better for you. Even if you use no pesticides on them, wash your vegetables before eating because city air contains toxic materials.

Dig Digging

You should like digging to be a successful gardener—even though, once you get your garden soil in good condition, mulching greatly decreases the need to disturb the soil. Mulching also saves water, which saves money. Soil that hasn't been worked for years will be packed down so solidly that nothing much can grow in it. To turn unworked earth into a garden, you have to spade it over thoroughly, down as deep as your spade can reach. Dig in fertilizer or manure and some compost, like rotted leaves and twigs, or peat moss to keep the soil from packing down again. Numerous active worms are a sign of good soil.

Plant Fruit Trees

Fruit trees take about five years to produce fruit, but once they do you can harvest wonderful fresh fruit for years with hardly any effort. Bare-root fruit trees are inexpensive and there's something particularly satisfying about planting a tree. You can usually buy them at discounts of 50% off at the end of the planting season. They still grow.

If you are lucky to have established trees, they're likely to produce more fruit than you and your friends can eat. You can dry the excess and wrap it in a fancy jar; it makes a wonderful gift. Fruit can be dried on wire mesh racks laid in the sun on a roof and protected by screen or cheesecloth from birds and insects. If you are careful you can dry fruit in your oven. Electric drying machines are also available.

You can also make jams and wines from your fruit. In fact, you can make many Christmas gifts as well as having lots of treats to give friends—all for practically no money.

Make Fertilizer

The fertility of your garden greatly increases when you return your biodegradable kitchen wastes back into it. The process is simple and the results can be astonishing. The easiest procedure is to establish a trench in some part of your garden that needs soil improvement, about a foot deep and a couple of feet long. Deposit kitchen scraps and lawn clippings in one end of the trench. As it fills, extend the trench a foot or so, shoveling the dirt you dig up onto the garbage deposited. This process gradually covers quite a lot of area in a year, and the deep digging produces great improvement in the garden soil.

Composting

A composting bin can be built of salvaged or scrap lumber, or simply by making a 3-feet-across cylinder of chicken-wire or snow-fence. For a four-person household, a bin three feet square and three feet high is usually adequate to accommodate kitchen wastes, grass clippings, gathered leaves, animal or chicken manure, dead annual plants, and so on. Use a plastic sheet for a cover to prevent the development of a fly population and increase the compost's temperature, which speeds decomposition and reduces odors.

Composting requires dampness, so occasionally sprinkle some water onto the pile. Periodically stirring up the mixture with a pitchfork helps the composting process along. An opening panel at ground level permits you to shovel out the finished material, which will be soft, loose, and pleasant-smelling. Alternatively, build the bin without a bottom, and remove finished material by blocking it up slightly.

Another method is to use an old metal or plastic garbage can. Punch a few holes near the bottom to provide air and cut off the bottom, so you can remove finished material later. Composting wastes can be mixed into soil or simply spread on your garden and dug in.

14

Grow Decorative Plants

Even the drabbest apartment looks better with flower pots on the windowsill. Living plants always make people feel good. Plants also give off oxygen during the day; that can't hurt either.

Start With Easy Plants

Most indoor plants are easy to grow. There's the conventional rubber plants and philodendrons, of course, but also try ferns and ivy. Sometimes you can find good ivy in an outdoor garden. Just put the stem in water and it will sprout, then plant it. Soon you have a beautiful house plant—for free.

Containers can be improvised from large painted tin cans or wooden boxes. Most plants need to be near windows but not in hot sun. If they need more light, paint the wall behind them white, or put a mirror there.

Grow Trees Indoors

You can grow small trees indoors. Trees are sometimes cheaper than a big potted flower plant. They need a lot of water, however, and do best if you keep the room temperature moderate. Get advice at a nursery. *Ficus benjamina* is one species that grows well indoors.

Buy Live Christmas Trees

Many people buy small live evergreens at Christmas, instead of cut trees. After New Year's, you get to plant it in your yard or in a park or along the street somewhere. Evergreens can tolerate a week in a heated house if you put them in the coolest spot—usually next to a big window—and are careful to keep their roots moist at all times.

A live Christmas tree smells nice and accords with the reverence for life that many of us wish to express at Christmas time. Nurseries can give you detailed advice about planting the tree. Remember that a small tree will someday be enormous, with powerful roots, so don't plant it right next to your house. If you do make this mistake, let the tree grow for a few years and then ceremonially cut it for your family Christmas tree. Alternatively, you can plant the tree in a large wooden container that you keep on your deck or in the yard; you bring the tree in year after year for Christmas. Soon the tree is like a member of the family.

Grow Vegetables for Their Beauty

Traditionally, people have been reluctant to mix decorative and edible plants. But edible plants can be quite beautiful. Asparagus, for instance, makes an attractive fern-like shrub after you have your fill of its springtime shoots. Artichokes and rhubarb offer dramatic garden accents. Beans, peas, and some squash can be trained on trellises to give privacy or shade. Strawberries and New Zealand spinach provide ground cover plus edibility. Nasturtium leaves add a tangy taste to salads. Alfalfa is a hardy, pleasant-looking plant that can feed rabbits; the sprouting seeds can be eaten yourself. There are also plants native to your region that the original inhabitants used for food. Growing them is a stylish challenge enjoyed by members of native plant societies; see if one exists nearby. Save room for a spice garden; fresh spices are more flavorsome than dried.

15

Raise Live Food

Fishing, hunting, and gathering are primordial survival techniques of human beings, and there is something to be said for staying in touch with them. In addition, they offer good opportunities not only to save money but also to make money.

Catch Fish

Even heavily urbanized areas often have good fishing spots quite close by. However, check with your health department about possible pollution hazards in local fish.

Catching fish is not easy, and you need to be instructed by someone who is experienced. Find a mentor to take you to places where people catch fish suitable for eating. Other aquatic creatures are delicacies in fancy restaurants: crayfish, crabs, and even frogs can be speared with a long pole or netted.

Every state requires a fishing license. Certain spots, like piers built with federal money, are exempt from licenses.

Raise Chickens

Chicken-raising is legal in most areas, but surprisingly few people take advantage of this as a source of low-cost protein—both meat and eggs. It can also be fun, and highly informative to children. If your chickens produce too many eggs for your own use, you can barter with them or give them to friends.

Raising a few chickens takes very little cash or time. The chickens can use up kitchen scraps that you wouldn't compost, like meat scraps, oyster shells, and various other kinds of refuse. Six hens can keep the average family in eggs most of the time. If you have a yard with long grass, they will consume bugs and grass and weed seeds, and will look sleek and beautiful. Like people, chickens do not thrive in confinement.

To get started in chicken raising, obtain guidance from your local Cooperative Extension office if you don't have a friend to instruct you. In order to raise chickens in town, you need to provide a securely fenced yard, secure from marauding dogs, with a wire-roofed sleeping pen to keep out raccoons. Avoid having roosters, whose crowing will probably be considered a public nuisance by your neighbors. Hens seem to be happy—and lay eggs—without them.

Sweeten Your Life with Bees

The term "busy little bees" describes these amazing beings well. Bees are incredibly industrious and, if you provide them a decent home, they will forage ceaselessly for you and provide large amounts of delicious honey for practically no cost, almost anywhere, except in agricultural areas with heavy pesticide use. Bees are legal to keep in most areas.

Bees can even be raised in indoor hives. A hive can be attached to sit on a windowsill, so long as the bee entrance is a bee-tight pipe; it can even have a glass wall—covered with a flap because bees don't like light in their hives—so that you can look in on them—which is really fun, especially for kids. A beehive can fit on many urban balconies. Beware, however, of locations near other people's balconies or windows, since bees returning at dusk are attracted by light.

Bees produce honey, a delicious and healthy sugar substitute and food-energy source, at the same time that they pollinate many plants, including fruit trees. People sometimes have an unreasonable fear of bees, but if a hive is in a backyard away from pedestrian traffic, it poses no danger to residents or passers-by. Your dog, if you have one, will soon learn to keep away from it. A careful beekeeper rarely gets stung.

Your local college or adult school may offer a course in beekeeping and your library certainly has instruction books. Best of all, however, is to find a beekeeper nearby who is already doing it and apprentice yourself for a while.

Have a Fish Pond

Having a pond in your yard can be a lot of fun. You might even install a small waterfall. The sound of moving water inspires mediation and it produces negative ions, which are said to have a positive effect on mood and health. It is possible to develop a small home-made windmill to run a pump to aerate and filter fish-pond water. Bluegills will thrive in such a pond but you may want to experiment with more exotic species, like tilapia and carp. Even if your area is urbanized, it should have a county agricultural agent who can give advice on ponds. In rural areas, a pond can be bigger and supply not only fish but water for fire-fighting.

If you also have a bee hive, you'll quickly learn that bees have a short lifetime. All around any busy hive will be a lot of dead bees. Fish love dead bees, which can constitute a large part of their diets. It is a good idea to put your beehive next to your fish pond.

16

Get Around Car-Free

Living closer to your job and main shopping is the biggest way to cut down on transportation time and money for stylish living.

Carpool

See if your employer's personnel office organizes carpools. In many small carpools, driving and use of car is rotated among members. In larger ones, a driver is hired. There are carpools where hot coffee is provided in the morning and snacks are shared on the way home. Like buses, carpool and vanpool vehicles are entitled to use special "diamond" auto lanes through congested points on highways, which makes your trip to work substantially faster than if you drove your own car, and you save tolls and parking expenses, too.

Take a Taxi

Taxis are fun to ride in. You can enjoy yourself with your friends in the back seat, or just watch the world go by. Taxis seem expensive. The question is whether they're really more expensive than other ways of getting around. You may be better off not owning a car and using taxis instead. If you calculate what your car really costs you to operate, that amount per month buys a surprising number of taxi rides. Of course, if you drive around on little trips all the time, you may find it hard to get cabs quickly. But if you plan your trips sensibly and phone for a taxi, it can work out well. When you use taxis you don't have to worry about whether your car is dependable for an important trip, or about car repair bills or where to park.

Many larger cities have subsidized dial-a-ride taxi or van services for seniors and handicapped people. Phone your city or county offices to find out what's available.

Take Public Transportation

If you're a sociable sort who is curious about people, you may find riding the bus more interesting than sitting all by yourself in your car. Call your transit system and ask for a free schedule and map of their lines. Study the map and mark the location of your house, your job, and wherever else you go a lot—clinic, school, supermarket, downtown. Determine if there are direct lines that run from near where you are to near where you want to go. If there's no direct line, call the transit information number again. Tell them where you are and where you want to go, and they will tell you the best route. Be ready to write down what they say.

You may occasionally wonder if riding public transportation is worth it. There are many things that will put public transit into perspective. Just owning a car involves certain unavoidable costs: purchasing, insuring, and maintaining. Dedicated use of public transportation can relieve you of the need to own a car. But even if you own a car, each trip costs you money: fueling and parking. In some cities, the hassle of parking alone out-weighs the hassle of using public transportation.

Ride a Motorcycle

Some people ride two-wheeled motor vehicles for economy and convenience, but many get hooked on the sheer excitement of it. You are also, of course, in more peril of injury—four times more peril than when traveling in a car. But there are benefits. You can park between buildings, between cars, under stairways or porches, and sometimes on the edge of sidewalks. Unlike riding a bicycle, you can carry a passenger with you. Riders of really big bikes, whose engines have more than a thousand cubic centimeters, say there's nothing like them for speed, comfort, and the pure joy of movement.

A light motorcycle is by far the cheapest fast motorized transportation around. Gas expenses are far less than for any car. A light machine with an engine displacement of 125 cubic centimeters or less will easily keep up with town traffic. A slightly larger machine will handle the highways.

Consider a Moped

Mopeds get fantastic mileage, can be parked in bicycle racks or on the sidewalk, and will keep up with street traffic. And if all else fails, they can be pedaled.

They're generally user-repairable and their operating costs are small. Such light bikes are safer than scooters, which are less stable because of the smaller tires.

Ride a Bike

A good bike can last you for decades making the cost per month very low, even for an expensive model. The best bike is light enough that you can pick it up with one hand and hoist it on your shoulder which makes it easy to carry up steps, into buildings, and onto light-rail or train cars.

Two designs predominate: *mountain bikes* which have wider tires and are good for riding on pot-holed streets, and *touring bikes,* meant for long-distance and high-speed riding on roads. The traditional 3-speed commuter bike with a coaster brake is still the world standard and works fine here too.

Repair it Yourself

Bikes need very few repairs. You can easily fix everything except gearshift problems, and even these are relatively cheap to have fixed in a shop. Buy a bike-fixing guidebook and you will spend virtually nothing on repairs—a pleasant change from car ownership. Bike shops sometimes have workshops on bike repair and maintenance.

Car-Bike Combo

Combining a bike with a car gives you a drive-then-ride flexibility that can be very useful if you have a parking problem near your job. Racks can be bought that clamp onto car bumpers and support a bike, or you can make such a rack yourself. Folding bikes that fit into a car trunk or closet are available and can be taken on trains. Many buses have bike racks.

Buy Cheap

There's a good secondhand market in bikes, especially on the bulletin boards around colleges and universities, where thousands of students own bikes and sell them when they leave town. If you buy new, Sears and Costco sell solid 3-speed models for a reasonable price.

Add Hauling Capacity

If you have a carrying basket on the front, you'll be able to haul at least one bag of groceries and larger baskets can be installed over the rear wheels to increase your hauling capacity. And for a small child, you can bolt a seat on the back, complete with a safety belt. These cost only a couple of dollars and kids love them.

Deter Theft

A beat-up bike is less likely to be stolen. This is an important consideration given that stealing a bike is easy work for anybody with a bolt cutter. Even the fantastic new locks can be defeated by a well-equipped thief. Better bikes now have removable wheels and seats to make them less attractive to thieves.

It's a good idea to register your bike, for a nominal fee, as insurance against theft. Real insurance can be bought but it's expensive.

Even if you lose a bike to thieves once in a while, you'll still be saving money. After I had a new bike for two years, for example, I calculated that compared to taking the bus to work, I had saved five times what the bike cost. At this rate I could have the bike stolen twice a year and still be ahead.

Use Your Feet

You can start out simply by walking to a few of the places you usually go to by car or bus. Then try a slightly different route. You'll probably be surprised at all the things you notice. Don't be in a hurry. Do your first walking when you can afford to stroll and loll a little, so that you don't resent the fact that it takes longer to "get somewhere" than if you were on wheels.

Check out your own walking range. If your present comfortable range is only a couple of blocks, extend it little by little. After a while, you'll identify your own style of walking. Some people walk fast; some dawdle. Some stop a lot; some keep moving. Some walkers like best to walk in the rain, or at night, or with their dogs. Some only like to walk where there are trees or water. Some find "nature walks" dull and walk only on busy city streets. Try out the different possibilities to discover your style.

Walking lets you use your body vigorously for what it so beautifully evolved for. With our American "practicality," we've come to think of walking only as a means to an end—to get somewhere. But walking is also an end itself: the enjoyment of your body's potentialities. It's also a healty way to burn up calories and lose weight.

17

Car Buying for Less

When you begin your search for a car, whether new or used, go to your local public library and study the car ratings in *Consumer Reports*. Talk to friends who have the kind of car you're thinking of getting. Ask about their service records and availability of good and reasonably priced service.

New Car Buying Tips

New-car prices are inflated and generally dealers expect to come down. Begin bargaining not from the sticker price but from the dealer's invoice price, available from *Consumer Reports* by fax, and the American Automobile Association offices. Also walkicheck the Internet for price comparisons. Once you know what the car is really worth, shop around and you will probably save several hundred dollars from a dealer eager to sell.

In the course of looking at cars you may test drive cars at a few dealers. Some of them will get information from you before letting you test drive. Be careful because they may be running a credit check on you. This is a problem because the credit rating companies keep a record of *each* request. In the course of looking for a new car, this could happen 3-4 times. Later, when you are applying for a home loan, for example, you will have to explain, in writing, each of these requests. In some cases it could cause you to have to pay a quarter percent higher interest rate on your home loan.

Buy Stripped Down

New cars come with a lot of expensive "options" that you probably don't need or want, such as jump seats, roof racks, and power windows. Many large dealers offer stripped-down models at substantial savings. These cars have all the essential features but not the unnecessary stuff. After you have identified the specific car and dealer price you want, check the big display car ads in the Sunday paper, looking for those offering the car you want for the lowest price. These are probably stripped down. Alternatively, you can call larger dealers and ask if they have any stripped down models in the car you want.

Getting the Deals

If you look at the big display car ads in the Sunday paper, you'll see that there are a few popular cars listed at a lower price than anywhere else. Often it will say something like, "three at this price" and list the engine numbers, which is required by consumer laws. The problem is that by the time you get to the dealer those three deals have been sold and the same car costs more for you. Here's a trick for getting one of those cheaper cars. Buy the Sunday paper on Saturday evening. When you find an ad for a reduced price on the car you want, go straight to the dealer the day before, on Saturday night. If the car is on the lot and advertised, they have to sell it to you at that price. It doesn't matter that it is the next day's paper.

Another way to save one or two thousand dollars, and sometimes even more, is to buy late in December when the dealers are anxious to dump the current year's cars. This is when you can really wheel and deal. If you are a good negotiator, you can walk away with a deal. If you can't get a good price at the first place, go to another dealer.

Tips on Buying Used Cars

A small, clean, used car, bought after careful inspection by a knowledgeable mechanic, will give you the most transportation for your money, and the least aggravation with repairs.

Find out the going price for the car you want before you begin your search. "Blue-book" fair prices for used cars can be found in your library's reference room and on the Internet. *Consumer Reports* rates used cars for their reliability—their charts contain some interesting surprises.

Buy From Private Parties

Generally, it is wisest to buy used cars from a priavte party, preferably an original owner living in an upscale area because they are more likely to have taken better care of the car and more likely to price the car low. It is harder to have your mechanic inspect cars on a dealer's lot. Private individuals, on the other hand, rarely object to mechanic inspections. Dealers usually price their used cars higher than do private individuals and it is easier to get non-dealers to come down in price.

Ask the seller why they are selling. Best are single-owner cars whose owners bought it new and did all of the recommended maintenance on schedule. Ask to see the maintenance and repair statements. Review them and ask the seller about any repairs that concern you.

If you do purchase from a dealer, make sure that you get a decent warranty in writing. Ask for 90 days or more. Whenever salespeople ask you to sign something, it is probably some kind of contract. Get a cup of coffee, sit down, and read everything carefully. If they pressure you, say you want to take it home to study it and show it to your sister-in-law who's a lawyer.

Inspect Used Cars Thoroughly

Have a mechanic look over the car. Most mechanics will give you a reasonably accurate opinion for a modest fee. Don't even consider buying a used car if the seller won't let you consult a mechanic. A mechanic can make tests you can't do yourself. If you're a member of the American Automobile Association, you can use their diagnostic service in major cities. If repairs are needed, but you want the car anyway, get the mechanic to write down exactly what they are. Use the list to negotiate a lower price.

Always Road Test

Whether it is a new or used car, always road test it before buying. Amazing as it may sound, about two-thirds of car buyers have not actually driven the car first. Any car you're discouraged from testing is probably a lemon.

Does the car accelerate well at both highway and street speeds? If not, it may need a tune-up or much more. Does it shimmy? This points to alignment or tire trouble. Does it tend to drift off to one side or the other if you lift your hands slightly off the wheel? This may indicate that the front-end is out of alignment. Push on the brakes gently. Do they pull in one direction, indicating bad brakes on that side? Does the car brake evenly at high speeds? Some squeaking of disk brakes is normal, but it can indicate problems if the car has drum brakes.

Beware of Salvaged Cars

Some unscrupulous people buy wrecked cars at insurance auctions, reconstruct them, and sell them to unsuspecting folks as good roadworthy cars. Sometimes halves of two wrecked cars are welded together. In fact, more than 10% of the used cars for sale are "salvaged," which means that they were considered "totaled" and sold for parts. Be suspicious if the seller insists on registering the car for you. You may have purchased a wrecked vehicle and the seller doesn't want you to see the title. When a car is salvaged, it is noted on the title or "pink slip." Always read the title very carefully. If you see the word "salvage," don't buy that car because it was wrecked and sold for salvage.

A car that's been wrecked can look perfect to the eye but still have its frame bent out of line so that the rear wheels don't exactly follow the front wheels—instead they run off to one side a little. This makes the car unsafe and also causes terrible tire wear. You can spot this by having someone drive the car straight away from you. A car that doesn't set level probably has a broken spring—another dangerous condition.

18

Reduce Car Ownership Costs

Overall, about 40% of Americans don't own a car. This is not so surprising when you realize that many people who do own a car find themselves spending a quarter or even more of their income on it.

Identify True Costs

Think of the purchase price in two ways to uncover its true economic reality. First, if you borrow the money to buy the car, and most people do, you need to add the interest you will pay to the sales price. Second, the money you're putting into the car could be in the bank, a money fund, or real estate investment, and growing in value; when you put money into the car, it immediately begins to "depreciate" or lose value. A new car can depreciate more than 20% the moment you drive it off the dealer lot, and about 10% per year thereafter. That's why it's generally more cost-effective to buy a two to three year old car, so long as you get one in good condition.

The total cost of owning and operating your car is probably much more than you suspect, and alternatives to driving make good sense economically and ecologically. Over the lifetime of the car, your insurance bill can cost you as much as the car itself, even if you have an old clunker and carry nothing but basic liability. Repair bills can cost more than you expect. A new car should be free of repair costs for the first two to four years, which is one advantage of buying new. Used cars, on the other hand, have more repair bills which usually add up to more than gas, oil, and tires. If you can do your own work, you can cut down repair expenses by maybe half. But don't kid yourself: modern cars are so computerized that they are pretty difficult for the home mechanic to repair.

Gas, oil, and maintenance costs, like tune-ups and oil changes, add up too. People who have cars drive a surprising amount. Average America drivers put in around 12,500 miles a year.

Other expenses include licenses and fees. Even if your car is so old it's down to the minimum rate, licenses cost something. Your driver's license has to be renewed periodically for a fee. You spend money on parking lots and meters, bridge and highway tolls, and perhaps even tickets.

One cost many overlook is theft. Car thieves can open a locked car in about 15 seconds to steal things from you and, of course, the car itself could disappear. Vandals may crack windows, tear off radio antennas, remove hubcaps, or steal tires.

Cut Operating Expenses

Figure your expenses out on a monthly or yearly basis. Gas is the most obvious expense, but many others add greatly to the cost of operating a car.

Save on Gas

To cut gas consumption, get regular tune-ups, drive at lower speeds, turn off the air conditioner, accelerate gently, and don't idle the engine for more than a few minutes if you can turn it off. The smaller, lighter, and more streamlined a car, the less gas it uses. Roof racks cause air resistance which lowers mileage. An air conditioner cuts mileage about 15%, so run it only when you really need it.

Do Regular Maintenance

Regular tuning of your engine increases gas mileage by about 10%. Replacing spark plugs and distributor points on older cars is easy and cheap. Reduce engine wear with regular oil and filter changes. This is easy to do yourself. Setting the engine's timing takes skill, but many drivers do it themselves—and so can you.

Drive Slower

Drive at a steady speed. Avoid jackrabbit starts, sudden braking, and unnecessary idling. Don't open windows unnecessarily when driving at high speed because it creates drag and cuts mileage, sometimes as much as an air conditioner does.

Save on Oil

Short-trip driving is the worst way to treat an internal-combustion engine. Oil doesn't lubricate well until the engine is really hot. Heat-control valves and automatic chokes tend to get stuck which increases the tendency of old engines to drip gas down into the crankcase where it dilutes the oil and forms corrosive acids. Cold engines also give lower mileage.

Proper lubrication and oil changing can double the lifetime of the engine. Engine wear will be cut down if you use "multigrade" oil, which is labeled "10W-30", or "10W-40". Stay away from additives—they won't save as much as they cost you. If you change your own oil, make sure to properly dispose of it.

Buy the Right Tires

Radial, steel-cord tires last about twice as long as nylon or rayon tires when they are used with the proper amount of air in them. They are more resistant to heavy impacts, and because they take low air pressure they have a larger "footprint" to hold better on the road. Radials also roll easier and thus improve gas mileage by several miles to the gallon. Their disadvantages are that they cost more and that they make a little louder hum on the road. Do not mix radials and bias-ply tires on your car because this will cause handling instability.

Buy Good Recaps

A recap should run almost as long as a new tire before it wears out, but it costs only half to two-thirds as much to purchase. Quality is a consideration because cheap retreads tend to wear rapidly, or may throw off the new rubber entirely while driving. Your car is only as safe as its tires. If you have a blow-out, you can get into a serious accident. Buy recaps only through a shop you trust. A good recapping retailer will give you a written guarantee.

Tires wear a little differently on different wheels, so periodic rotating is generally recommended. Don't rotate a new spare—save it, so that you'll only need three new tires when the time comes.

Buy the Right Battery

Short, around-town driving seldom gives a battery the chance to get fully recharged. If that's your main kind of driving, spend a little more and get a high-quality battery. The strength of a battery is measured in "ampere hours," and dealer charts indicate which batteries have the right rating for your car. For cold-weather starting, you'll need the full rating power. Usually, big automotive parts stores have the best deals.

Do Routine Maintenance Yourself

You can gain skill at diagnosing what's wrong with your car and probably fix common small problems. Many evening schools offer do-it-yourself auto-repair courses; some are especially set up for women. When you do take your car in, get a work-order sheet filled out that says what is to be done. Never sign a blank order sheet.

Walk or Bike

Save your car, save money, and save your health by leaving your car at home and walking or biking when it is a trip of a mile or two. You can park bikes anywhere—no need to drive around looking for a space or to spend money on a parking lot. A bicyclist often moves faster than a car driver, especially during rush hour.

19

Travel Cheaply

Getting out of town once in a while is refreshing to the spirit. Even if you are on a limited budget, you don't have to feel permanently stuck where you are. You can travel light and travel far on small amounts of money. The secret is to provide your necessities outside of hotels, motels, and restaurants. If you're traveling by car or truck or camper, arrange to sleep in it. Take along a stove to cook on and eat restaurant or fast food only on special occasions. Use state and national park campgrounds, especially when you need to take a bath and do the wash. Plan your route to avoid interstate highways as much as possible—find the old roads that wind around through interesting little towns where you can meet friendly people and learn how they live.

Take the Train

Trains are far more energy-efficient than cars or trucks, and this often translates into cheaper fares for you. Besides, you get the experience of riding in huge, comfortable seats in a large space where you can move around. You can go find a cup of coffee, and see scenery invisible from highways even if you could afford to take your eyes off the road. Every other industrialized country has convenient and rapid train service, and we still have some vestiges of it with Amtrak.

You can sometimes find a train going where you want to go, and if getting there on time is not too important to you, give it a try. Phone Amtrak for schedules and ticket prices. Be sure to bring along sandwich makings, fruit, and other food to keep eating expenses down. Otherwise you'll pay plenty in the dining car or at the vending machines.

If you know of picturesque places along the way, stopovers are often possible. But just being on a train is a stress-free experience, and if you're feeling sociable you can chat comfortably—unlike being drowned out by airplane noise.

Take the Bus

Bus lines reach most places in the country, even the tiniest, and they're cheap. Long-distance buses have more spacious seating than airplanes, clean restrooms, and are non-smoking. They provide a soft, comfortable ride, and bus stations are usually in convenient central locations. In planning a bus trip, find out whether there are express buses to where you want to go. You can stop off repeatedly on a bus ticket. So it is a fun way to travel if you want to see some places along the route. Take along food to save money and avoid bus-stop greasy spoons.

A lively alternative to regular bus service is Greentortoise Adventure Bus Travel. Their motto is

"Arrive inspired, not dog tired." Greentortoise provides clean, comfortable, and fun busing—often they stop for communal cookout meals, a dip in a creek, or a long sauna. The buses convert into bunks for all during "sleep over" stops, where everyone brings a sleeping bag and stretches out for a comfortable night's sleep. Based in San Francisco, Greentortoise has main routes up and down the West Coast, to Yosemite, Yellowstone, the Baja peninsula, Alaska, and even to the East Coast. This is not for the pampered traveler—or people who don't appreciate music playing most of the time. But Greentortoise is adventurous travel for those who want to pay less, enjoy the trip more, and get friendly with those they're traveling with.

Hitchhike

Hitchhiking at one time was the cheapest and in some ways the most interesting way to travel—and it still is in many parts of the world. Unfortunately, hitchhiking has become dangerous in the US. Nevertheless, plenty of people still enjoy this adventuresome way of traveling elsewhere. With a pack on your back and a sleeping bag, you can be as footloose and fancy-free as it's possible for a human being to be. You'll find hostels and other lodgings favored by hikers and hitchhikers in most of the scenic regions of the world.

Travel by Bike

Bicycling is a healthy and exciting way to travel. You see more and learn more. In the words of a wise old geographer, Carl Sauer, "Locomotion should be slow, the slower the better; and should be often interrupted by leisurely halts to sit on vantage points and stop at question marks."

You can carry a lot more weight on a bike than on your back, as well as go a lot faster, so biking makes sense for covering large scenic areas. Bike clubs, though they're mostly oriented to local trips, sometimes organize long-distance rides. Find them through a good bike shop.

Try Drive-a-Ways

If you have a driver's license and seem responsible, you can sometimes get cars from a drive-away agency listed in the Yellow Pages under Automobile Transporters and Drive-Away Companies or in newspaper classified ads. Sometimes you have to pay for the gas, but often not. Ask about the insurance situation and clarify what to do if the car breaks down. This can be the fastest, cheapest, and most scenic way to get from one major city to another.

Try Courier Flights

Courier companies exist to provide more rapid and secure delivery of goods or documents than can be offered by regular shipping outfits. These companies need passengers to accompany packages to places all over the world, and so offer people over 21 years old an opportunity to fly at a much reduced fare. The packages take the place of your luggage; so while your own baggage has to be limited, this gives you the chance to go to places you never could have afforded. Generally, it costs about half of the usual fare. Contact the International Association of Air Travel Couriers which you can find on the internet. They charge a nominal membership fee and provide daily updates of air courier trips.

20

Find Cheap Lodging

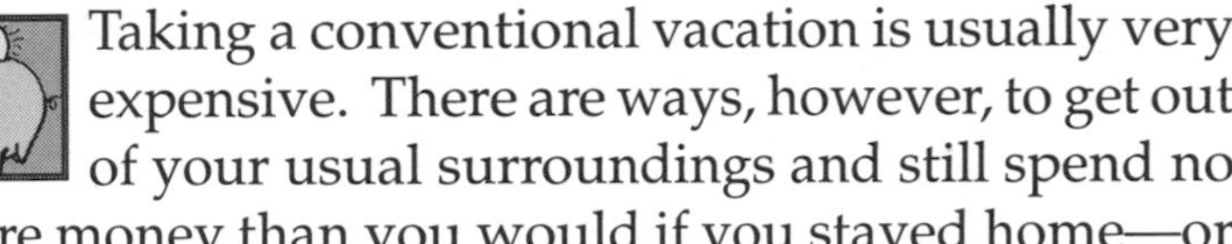

Taking a conventional vacation is usually very expensive. There are ways, however, to get out of your usual surroundings and still spend no more money than you would if you stayed home—or maybe less.

Camp Out

There are many public camping grounds in the United States, especially in the West. Unfortunately, during peak season they are crowded and noisy. Your best bet is to go against the flow and use parks in off-season months. Concentrate on the national forests. There are some camping areas with toilet and water facilities, but camping away from the roads is usually permitted anywhere you can find a suitable site. The only regulations usually concern fire permits.

Detailed maps showing established campsites are available from National Forest Service offices in Washington, D.C. and in many other cities, and at forest headquarters. These maps show the many dirt roads and trails that lead off into remote regions where only hardier backpackers penetrate—and where you'll be free of the clusters of pickup campers, generator rigs, and other perils that infect popular campgrounds.

Astonishingly enough, walking a mile is plenty to get away from the crowds and may well bring you to some idyllic lake, meadow, stream bank, or other pleasant spot. Buy the US Geological Survey "quadrangle" map of the general area you're interested in. Specialized map stores or recreational equipment stores sell them. They're also available in the park visitor's center. Study the dirt roads that lead into the wilderness in interesting directions. Be willing to spend some time exploring an area. Once you get to know it, you may find wonderful places you will want to come back to next year and the year after that. With your map and a compass you can strike out across country to campsites further away from the roads and to other points of interest, like lookouts and hot springs.

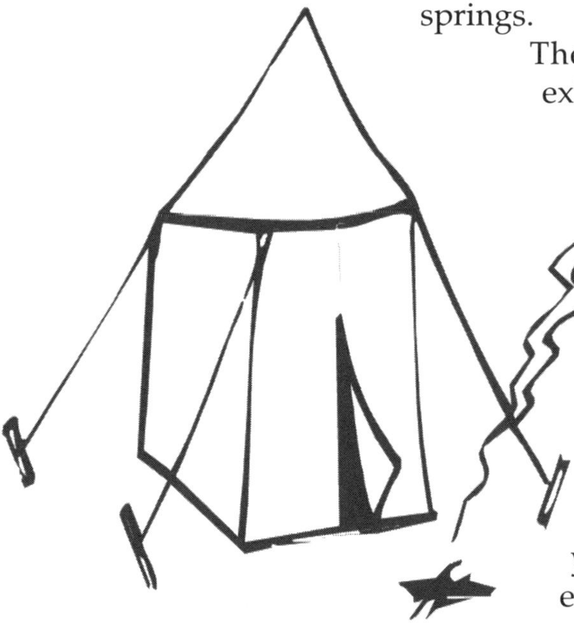

There's something exhilarating about carrying everything you need for a week on your back and being free to go wherever your feet take you. But for such a venture, you need proper equipment and some experience in overnight camping. It's best to borrow the equipment for your first time, just in case you don't like it.

It's surprisingly easy to get lost when you're a beginning hiker. It is smart to go with experienced hikers and learn their tricks. Living outdoors is invigorating, but if you don't learn how to do it right, you'll wear yourself out and irritate everybody around you. The greatest thing about camping is the utter lassitude that settles over you once you've laid out your camp—and you want to be able to enjoy that to the fullest.

Sleep in a Van or RV

Vans and RVs get low mileage so it generally isn't economically feasible to use one as your main mode of transportation. On the other hand, when you consider that you are driving your "house" around and can sleep for free—then they can be a great deal for a road trip, especially if there are two or three or more of you traveling. You might be able to rent or make a trade of some sort with a friend who owns an RV for a couple of weeks for your vacation.

Generally, you can stop overnight anywhere that is not posted otherwise, as long as you sleep *inside* the vehicle. This means that you can easily stay near beaches, lakes, and other attractive spots. You can also park in RV camps, which have amenities like swimming pools and washing machines, but they are often crowded and more expensive than you'd guess.

Exchange Houses

You can sometimes arrange to switch houses with people who live in other parts of the country, or even in foreign countries, giving both of you a cheap vacation. You can find people by placing an ad in a publication read by the kind of people you'd like to exchange with, or in the local paper of the place you want to visit. There are international directories of people offering house exchanges. Try the International Home Exchange Network in Longwood, Flordia, or Green Theme International which can be found by search the internet by their name

In an exchange vacation, you may be able to get near some gorgeous scenery you've always wanted to see or live in a city you've always wanted to visit or on a houseboat without the hassle of baggage and the expenditure of a lot of money.

Take a Work Vacation

Young people, especially, can sometimes arrange summer jobs at ranches, orchards, resorts, and other establishments that need seasonal help. Concessionaire companies that run facilities in national parks recruit students every year. Find such possibilities through personal contacts—parents, friends, and relatives. Employment agencies and ads sometimes help. Talk to people in ski-equipment stores, for example, if you want to spend some time working in the mountains during the ski season.

If such inquiries don't turn up anything, just go to the area you're interested in well before the season and nose around, asking advice from the permanent residents. "Ecotourism" where you travel to another culture and do ecologically useful work is increasingly popular. Check for ads in environmental magazines.

Stay in Hostels

Hostels are generally stripped-down accommodations that cost less than motels. They usually offer a bed, toilet, shower or bath, and sometimes shared cooking facilities. The YMCA or a similar organization usually runs hostels. They generally have a greater variety of people using them than in earlier times when their clientele was made up mainly of penniless students on backpacking tours. Contact the American Youth Hostels in San Francisco for more information.

Carry a Sleeping Bag

A sleeping bag or bedroll can liberate you from a bed, the nest, as a permanent structure to which you must return every night. It makes the whole world a possible sleeping place. With your bag strapped to your back, on your bicycle rack, or thrown into the trunk of your car, you can camp just about anywhere, anytime—even at friends' houses.

Moreover, getting children used to sleeping bags makes them far more portable than children used to sleeping only in cribs or beds. You can take them with you to parties, visits, and long drives. If they're in their familiar bag, they'll sleep cozily.

Carry a Portable Stove

Portable propane-canister stoves are as easy to use as a stove in your house. It costs almost nothing to cook a meal on a camping stove using white gas and only slightly more with propane. An added advantage of having a camping stove around is to have it for emergencies like earthquakes or hurricanes so you can still cook when there is no power or gas.

If you're going backpacking, you'll need a really small, light stove. The Svea that burns white gas has a self-contained cooking pot and is reliable. Using it is tricky so practice starting and cleaning it before you go out with it. Primus makes a good alcohol-burning backpacker's stove. These tiny stoves generate a surprising amount of heat but you wouldn't want to do regular home cooking on one.

The Coleman brand name is one of the best stoves. They make better car-camping stoves than anybody else and they are usually cheaper. You can often pick up a good Coleman stove at a garage sale or second hand store. They're pretty safe to use and rarely break down.

21

Own Your Dwelling

Buying your home is a smart thing to do if you want to live cheaply with style. Federal and state tax laws let you deduct all of your mortgage interest and property taxes from your income. For the first ten to twenty years—depending upon the term and rates—your mortgage payment is almost all interest. It is an amazing amount. For example, a mortgage payment of $2000 can easily be $1850 interest! Let's say that you must pay 20% of your gross adjusted income to tax. As a deduction on your income tax, you would save $370 or more a month, or $4440 a year in taxes. This is how home ownership provides you with a "tax shelter."

So buy your home and let Uncle Sam help pay for it!

If you've never owned a home, you are probably eligible for special buyer terms under a "First Time Buyer" program sponsored by many cities to help people become home owners by providing lower down payment requirements, as low as 3% down, lower interest rates, and easier qualifying terms.

Buy, Don't Sell

A lot of people buy a modest house, a "starter home," and over years they outgrow it. Since they have built up equity, they can move on to a nicer, bigger home. So they sell the first one and buy the new home.

If you are thinking along these lines, think again. If you refinance the first home or use an equity loan, you can pull out much of your equity to use to purchase the second home. Then you rent your old house. This is smart because your old house is the best rental for a beginning landlord. You know the house and its quirks. You know the neighbors, who will keep an eye on it for you. Your old house is low risk and you already own it. Banks want bigger down payments and higher interest rates on rentals. But you don't have to qualify to buy this rental, because you already own it. Since you lived in it, you probably have the more favorable homeowner lending terms, and you don't have to inform the lender that you've moved!

Get a Second Home

The government allows you to deduct interest and taxes on two homes. If you can squirrel away enough funds, have an equity line of credit, or if you come into an inheritance, it might be smart to buy a second home, which will allow you to shelter even more of your tax dollars. This might be especially useful if you are an avid skier, for example. Instead of paying for motels, you could be paying the mortgage on a second home, and maybe rent it out when you're not using it. Alternatively, you can buy your retirement home now. You can use it initially as a weekend get-a-way and eventually move in full time. If you are in your higher earning years, you know prices will go up and it will cost a lot more later when you are ready to retire and have less income. But make sure to get good financial advice so you can set it up right.

Make a "Gypsy Wagon"

Ingenious and restless souls have discovered anew that a moveable house made from a bread truck or school bus has advantages. You can rove around, visiting your friends in the country or in the city, without having to ask them to put you up. You're never forced to eat out—your kitchen is always with you.

If you find a spot you like, you can usually stay for three nights without having to move to a new parking spot. Generally, you can park anywhere overnight, unless restrictions are posted. The immense areas of our national forests are open to your wanderings where you will likely encounter roving bands of "seniors" in their big RVs.

The government classifies mobile homes and recreational vehicles as "homes." RVs are expensive and when purchased with a loan, the interest can be high. If the RV has full living facilities and you use it as your "home," it can qualify as a second home and you can get big deductions and save a bundle on your taxes.

Buy a Multiple Unit Dwelling

Along the same lines, it makes a lot of sense to buy a duplex or a fourplex. If you have a duplex, you can live in one side and rent out the other. You have somebody else helping to buy the property for you, but you don't have to live with them as roommates. Surprisingly, duplexes usually cost only about ten percent more than a single family dwelling in the same neighborhood. The rent from the second unit will help you qualify for the loan. Yet, since the building will be owner-occupied, you will get the more favorable homeowner lending terms and rates.

You will get substantial additional tax deductions from the rental unit. You get depreciation deductions. In real estate, it is assumed that the building is wearing out and will be completely used up or "depreciated" in 27.5 years. Because the rental is an "income-producing" holding you are allowed to subtract, as a deduction from your income tax, the depreciation that occurs every year.

For example, suppose you purchased the duplex for $300,000. You can only depreciate the building, not the land because the land remains when the building has worn out. The property tax bill tells the specific breakdown, which is usually one third for land value and two thirds for improvement or building value. In our example, the building would be worth $200,000. Since you would be renting half, you could depreciate the half you rent or $100,000. Using the straight-line method which is the most conservative, you could deduct $3636 ($100,000 divided by 27.5 years) from your taxes each year for 27 years! That deduction could save you $1000 or more a year or about $100 a month in taxes. That's impressive.

The beauty of this is that you get to live in one side for half price. And you get to deduct depreciation, mortgage interest, property tax, and certain repair and improvement costs from your taxable income. Meanwhile, it is very likely that your duplex will actually gain in monetary value and that the rent will creep up. As the rent for your rental unit goes up, your personal housing costs go down.

Buy a Multiple Unit in Partnership

An alternative is to buy a multiple unit in partnership with someone else. Taking the same duplex, you and a colleague, friend, or family member, for example, could buy the property together. You each live very inexpensively, far cheaper than you would paying rent for a comparable unit. Over time, relative to market rents, your housing cost will remain reasonably constant, while surrounding rents will probably go up.

This type of arrangement is particularly beneficial when you have problem credit or not enough money for a down payment by yourself. A good partner who has better credit or more money can bolster your loan application and help you qualify. Be careful in choosing a partner, however, and make sure you write down your partnership agreement—particularly, what happens if one of you wants to sell. Another good idea, and a handy exercise, is for each partner to write a letter of understanding so it is clear to each partner what the other *thinks* the partnership agreement means.

Buy a Manufactured Home

Manufactured homes have oddball features that are beneficial to someone seeking an economical housing alternative, but also wanting style and comfort. Manufactured homes evolved from "mobile" homes and are still legally considered to be vehicles and must post a license plate like a car or truck. This means that the purchase loan is a "consumer" loan—virtually the same as a car loan. It is very easy to get and has the maximum consumer protection.

Because the house is supposedly mobile, it has metal wheels underneath and sits on blocks. You can convert it to "real estate" simply by having it installed on a foundation on a separate lot. Once done, it is no longer mobile, but a full-fledged house, and will qualify for a conventional bank home loan, which has a considerably lower interest rate.

You can arrange for everything at once. If you buy the house new, you can have the dealer clear your lot and install the foundation. All of these costs can be put into the same purchase loan. Generally, you have your home, ready to move into, in three to six weeks. This is one way to get a very inexpensive "vacation" home.

Manufactured homes are much less expensive so you get more for your money than in a "stick-built" house. They are amazingly fancy with spa-type bathtubs in the master bedrooms and vaulted ceilings—especially in the double- and triple-wide models. A big plus is that steel frame structures avoid dry rot and damage from termites and beetles.

Many towns that formerly turned up their noses at mobile or "manufactured" homes can no longer keep them out due to lawsuits by home manufacturers. If the dwelling meets local building codes, cities can not exclude them simply because they are "manufactured."

Manufactured homes are often used in residence park which tend to be more friendly and cooperative places to live. Units are sometimes for sale or rent.

Buy a Fixer-Upper

If you are handy, with carpentry, plumbing, and so forth—and brave—you can buy a fixer-upper. Look for a property in a good location that has some moderate to severe problems. This is the kind of property you can get at a bargain and often the owner will carry the loan, which saves you more money. If you can do the work and you can live in the dwelling at the same time, you can make out very well on a shoestring. If you are able to live in chaos when the kitchen is ripped out or the floors are half done, you can turn straw into gold. You can set yourself up in a situation where you can live cheaply with style for life.

Always Use a Title Company

Always go through a title company and always get title insurance—no exceptions. Title insurance usually costs 0.5% of the amount being insured. Title insurance on the full price of a $300,000 home would be $1,500. It is worth it. The title company guarantees that you have a "clean title," meaning clear ownership of the property. If anything turns up after the sale, such as a lien or easement, the title company pays to fix it.

Never buy real estate with a "quit claim" deed. This is where one person signs over the property to another person. The quit claim can be recorded for about $25. It is a legal transfer but you may have a "dirty" title. The person signing over the deed to you may sincerely believe that there is no problem. You can pay on a property for many years and then something could come out of left field and, in the worst case, you could lose your property. *Always* get title insurance. Don't scrimp here.

Create a Perpetual Income

There are lots of people who have no pension plans and only meager Social Security payments to support them in their senior years. Artists, writers, self-employed, divorced and widowed women, people inching by, and people who don't have IRAs. You can create your own perpetual pension payment.

Let's say years have gone by and you're a retired senior citizen. You've paid off the mortgages on both houses in the example above. You don't want the burden of managing your rental any more, but you need that monthly money. If you're like many seniors, your home feels too big and caring for it is too much work. Here's how to create an on-going income from those houses. You sell and "carry the paper," which means that you are the lender—there is no bank. You get the down payment, which is typically twenty percent, immediately. Plus, for the next twenty to thirty years, depending on the term of the mortgages, you will have a few thousand dollars flowing in every month, with virtually no effort, repairs, or tenant problems. Your payments can be automatically deposited. You can travel—at last—knowing the money is going into your account every month. If the buyer defaults on paying, your lawyers foreclose and you sell the property again.

Setting up this type of arrangement is very easy and inexpensive. A "title company" can do all the paper work and legal recordings for you. You don't need a lawyer, and you may well get a higher price; "owner will carry" deals, as they are called, are usually hard to find in cities and during boom economies.

22

Make Furniture

Furniture, especially handmade furniture, can cost a small fortune. If you have the abilities, making your own furniture will not only save you money, but also improve your quality of life. Even without much ability, there is much you can do.

Make Bookshelves

Most homes lack bookshelves, though they may have incinerators, dirty-clothes chutes, special silverware drawers, linen closets, and other storage facilities. A simple solution is the board-and-concrete-block system. You can use just about any kind of boards and they don't all have to be the same type, length, or even width. Varied, interesting wood is half the fun—driftwood, used construction lumber, old pieces of shelving. Large concrete blocks are more stable and cheaper than bricks, and the holes are useful for holding pencils, letters, chopsticks, rulers, and many other little things that won't fit into your drawers. Always build more bookshelves than you think you will need, because you'll soon fill the extra space with radio, stereo, disks, and boxes of small objects.

Make Your Own Couch

There are drawbacks to a standard couch. The person seated in the middle makes an obstruction so the end people can't talk to each other. A two-person "love seat" is better for conversational purposes. Many couches are too narrow or too lumpy to sleep on comfortably. Couches that fold out to make a bed can be convenient, but they're usually ugly, too stiff, or too saggy, and cost a fortune unless you can find one secondhand. They are also very heavy to move. Futons, which are cotton mats sewn together, are a healthier alternative. Plus, they save space by folding up either into a pile or with a wood frame into a couch.

If you want a really satisfactory couch, make your own. This is not difficult if you liberate your mind from the conventional ideas. What you are after, presumably, is something that you and your friends can sit on, lounge on, and sometimes sleep on. In short, a couch is a largish, more or less flat surface, with a back along one side to lean on. This, like a bed, can be achieved with a large piece of plywood, some two-by-four lumber to support it, slabs of foam rubber, an attractive large piece of cloth, and some throw pillows.

You can make it freestanding or build it into a corner—which is easier, since you don't need as many legs. You can make it low to the floor, or higher. Or you can hinge it at the back so it will tilt a bit for more comfortable seating and go down flat for sleeping. You could even make it fold up all the way against the wall, to make space for daytime activities. You can suspend a legless couch on ropes or cables from ceiling joist, so that it can gently swing back and forth. You can make a storage box under it, or even drawers.

Build Tables

Eating is the one activity that all people in a house should do together, which makes the dining table the real center of the household. Round tables have the great advantage of equally integrating everyone in the conversation. Their shape naturally tends to make people feel more together. The most stylish and ceremonious tables are made of heavy solid wood, mounted on stout legs or a base. If you cannot find a solid table big enough to comfortably seat all the people you like to feed, make one. Prefabricated bases are available inexpensively at home remodeling and finish-it-yourself furniture stores. Tops can be made from a variety of materials.

Refinish Used Furniture

Inexpensive, used furniture purchased from a thrift store or garage sale can often be given new life and charm with simple paint or varnish. Generally, look for chairs, tables, and other pieces that are made from solid wood, rather than pressboard covered with a veneer.

Give Old Chairs New Life

You can find good old kitchen chairs that are sturdy and beautiful. Instead of looking for a set, be happy with an assortment of beautiful different ones. Many old chairs have been coated with layer after layer of paint but are good solid wood underneath. Paint remover will take the paint off.

If you come across a really beautiful easy chair of simple design, you can reupholster it yourself. Study it carefully, however; the more of the covering attached with tacks, rather than by fitting and sewing, the easier it is to reupholster.

Antique it

One approach is to paint the piece with a basic color. Then use a second color to spiff it up. For example, you paint over a lighter base color with a diluted black or brown paint that is wiped off before it dries with paper towels. The darker paint stays in holes and scratches and leaves streaks. It gives a lovely antique look. There are many hobby books with ideas for inexpensive furniture refinishing.

Whitewash it

Whitewash, the ancient covering for many beautiful old country fences and barns, washes away very slowly and irregularly, leaving an extremely nice weathered effect. To make it, buy lime, fine-ground casein which is the main ingredient in white glue, ground kaolin which is white clay, and sodium carbonate—if you intend to use it outdoors. Approximate ratios for outdoor use: 32 ounces lime, 8 ounces casein, 6 ounces kaolin, and 1 ounce sodium carbonate. For indoors: 30 ounces lime, 3 ounces casein, and 20 ounces kaolin. Precise measurements aren't essential. Mix all the ingredients very thoroughly while dry, then add about half their volume of water. Stir until dissolved, and let stand half an hour before application.

Oil it

The soft, lustrous surface of the veranda planks in traditional Japanese houses comes from their being wiped down by hand over the years, so that a mixture of sweat oils gradually protects them. Linseed oil rubbed in will give wood a similar beautiful soft glow. Sculptures in New Guinea are polished with animal fats rubbed thoroughly into the wood. In fact, practically any kind of fat or oil will give wood a protective gloss. Hard rubbing closes the surface pores of wood slightly, making it less water-absorbent. If you don't like the raw look of newly sawed wood you can "paint" it with a mixture of earth and water; this darkens it and makes it look weathered.

Professional painters buy fine brushes and use them for years. For the person doing an occasional small paint job, such as a chair or table with oil or acrylic paint, it's cheaper to buy a throw-away paint brush, since you would spend at least as much buying the cleaning stuff.

23

Cheap and Classy Home Improvements

Sometimes an apartment can seem so appealing when you first walk in that you forget to check it thoroughly to see whether it really suits you. However, moving is expensive. After the expense of buying packing boxes and tape, you must pay to have your phone relocated, for example. Additionally, property owners tend to hold rents down for sitting tenants and take the opportunity to raise the rent when the unit is vacated. So it's likely that your rent is a little—or a lot—below the market if you've been living in your current place for a few years. When you move you'll probably pay more rent for the new place than the old tenant paid. So it is smart to make price comparisons before giving notice to your landlord. You might be saving money right where you are now! If you are, perhaps there's a way to freshen up your place so that it has a new home feeling—without actually moving.

Be Creative

When moving to a new place, instead of taking everything you own, bring only those things you really love and absolutely must have. Give the new place time to develop its own spirit.

Go to your new home with nothing but a cushion and just sit quietly for a while in each room, looking around. Notice how the light falls and what you see out the windows. Listen to the noises. Feel how the air circulates. See if you can judge what the place wants you to do with it. Would a little painting of cabinets or door and window trim give new life to the interior and link one room to another? Can you provide special places for the furniture you're bringing in, so that it will feel at home and not crowd you?

Practice Simple Living

It's easiest to make a house express you, when you take a simple-living approach. Strive for elegant simplicity—for lightness—for grace. Be aesthetically economical—which usually means being financially economical, too. In the long run, it is better to have a few really good things in your house than a hodgepodge of cheap stuff. A simple-living approach does not mean austerity or denying yourself pleasures; it means making sure that your pleasures are really satisfying, and that they are your own.

Real luxury consists in having the things you need and love around. If you treat your dwelling with this kind of careful respect, it will repay you with a sense of repose, shelter, and peace.

Bring nature inside. You may be sick of driftwood or shells, but the world is full of beautiful and mysterious leaves, sticks, rocks, moss, and other free stuff.

Bare is Beautiful

Bare walls can be beautiful. A plain wall, if it's a good color, can be restful and surprisingly interesting. Some people enjoy plastering walls with magazine-clipping pictures, calendars, free posters from travel agencies, outrageous newspaper headlines, and so on. Another approach is special effects painting with feathers, sponges, and other texturing "tools." It is inexpensive to do and looks like an upscale decorating job. Home improvement stores like Home Depot often hold free classes on this and other decorating techniques.

Uneven floors, or floors with a lot of cracks in the wood, can be covered with masonite, which is the cheapest possible covering. You can find rugs and carpeting pieces in thrift shops. If they're small and not too heavy and stiff, they can be dyed. An especially beautiful rug can be tacked on a wall that's cracked or peeling. Burlap and other kinds of inexpensive cloth can also be used as a wall covering or hanging.

Bare floors can be beautiful. Many old houses have either beautiful patterned hardwood floors or worn softwood board floors. It's a lot of work to restore such floors to good condition, but worth it, for they will be a pleasure to look at and walk on. You can rent powerful floor sanders from equipment rental places, and then varnish or oil the sanded wood. It's hard, dusty work but satisfying and cheaper than anything else you could do with your floor.

Use Wasted Space

You can transform a tiny, ugly apartment into one that feels spacious and looks lovely. If you live in a small space, take some tips from the Japanese, who have learned to live well in very jammed-in conditions. For the Japanese, spaces have multiple uses. For example, instead of a large space-gobbling dining room table, you might store a small table on top of a cabinet and only bring it down for meals. You might line the walls with storage cabinets, mounted high enough to keep the floor underneath free. Like the Japanese, you can bring out sleeping quilts and turn a general purpose room into a bedroom—or bring out pillows and it becomes an area where friends can sit and socialize.

Learn from boats, where there is a compact storage place for everything—if there weren't, stuff would roll all over the boat in a storm. The tiny living spaces in boats can be quite charming and romantic.

Sometimes you can change the shape of space in your house. Many interior walls are nonweight-bearing—they don't hold up the roof or the floor above—and can be removed. Sometimes you can knock the plaster off the studs or make an archway. A house feels more comfortable and interesting when you can see more than a few feet into it. A strategically placed mirror or window can also make a small room feel more spacious.

Don't forget the outside. A flat roof, for example, can be turned into a roof garden or sunbathing area. By building a fence out of recycled lumber or driftwood, you can make a private garden or play yard.

Suspending Things

Hardware stores are full of hooks, wires, rods, and bars of all sorts, but you almost never really need anything but nails or, more stylishly, dowels. If, for instance, you want to hang up something in a wooden cabinet, you can drill little holes in it, run strings or wires through the holes, and knot them inside. You accomplish three things by such an alternative to the conventional hook. You liberate yourself from the standard way of doing things, you keep ugly chrome-plate or plastic out of your house, and you save money.

Your imagination, once liberated, may lead you to do quite beautiful things. You may find yourself braiding colorful strings to hang up paper towels or toilet paper. Or you may use pieces of tree branch as coat hooks; build special racks of driftwood or scrap wood for spices or candles or writing materials; put small plants in the cavities of rocks; hang pots and pans from twisted pieces of very old rusty metal. Your imagination is the only limit.

Make a Sleeping Loft

The "bedroom" is actually a very recent invention, and it wastes a lot of scarce space. In old Dutch farmhouses, beds were built into the walls as alcoves, separated from the main room by a curtain that could be drawn when you went to bed. Modern counterparts of these alcoves usually have windows for ventilation and a view.

A loft bed should be high enough that cupboards or drawers fit under it so that both sleeping space and storage space can be provided in an area of about five by six feet. Such "roomette" bedrooms can be built with doors, of course, and with a little strip of floor space along the front where you can stand to dress.

Try Flexible Bed Areas

Sleeping places can be practically anywhere. You can hang them by chains or heavy ropes or wires from the roof. You can build them as little high-up balconies—surrounded by curtains if you like. You can make double-deckers or triple-deckers. One clever friend of mine put his bed over his sink. He reasoned that airspace over the sink was just going to waste—so he built a frame out of two-by-fours, nailed up a plywood sheet and a railing, built a little ladder, and had a loft-bed without wasting any floor space at all.

Enlarge Your Bathroom

After the kitchen, the bathroom is the most important room in the house. It's ridiculous that bathrooms are built hardly bigger than closets. See if yours might be enlarged by knocking out a wall, or perhaps adding a big bay-window alcove. A stylish bathroom not only has a comfortable, deep tub, it also has a shower and plenty of room for taking off clothes and for sitting around and reading. It should have a big window that looks out on trees and green things, or a view of some kind.

Bathe in Groups

What you mainly need for joyful bathing is plenty of hot water. Bathing with family or friends can be a pleasure while saving money on your water bill. Unfortunately, the standard American tub will barely accommodate two people.

You might build your own hot tub or pool. Build it on solid ground or over a reinforced part of the floor. Filled, it will weigh enough to break through an ordinary floor and flood whatever is below. Traditional wooden tubs are difficult to heat, maintain, and keep clean, however, so you might want to consider buying a modern hot tub. New hot tubs are very efficient. They operate on 110-watt power and are well insulated so they are economical to use.

An ample supply of clothes hooks makes it easier for several people to use the bathing facilities at once. Make sure there are plants—ferns especially love the moist air. Whether you prefer natural wood or brightly painted walls, a soft rug or a cool smooth floor, consider the bathroom a meditation chamber. The purpose of taking a bath is not only to get clean, but also to restore contact with our primal element. Make bathing an inexpensive and joyous occasion.

Improvise Don't Buy

The key is to be bold. Think big and you may come up with something really beautiful. There's always more than one way to do things, and sometimes the usual way is not the most attractive or interesting. By developing a sense of innovative and stylish design, you can build and fix things without a great deal of the usual money-eating expenses. Here are possible alternatives to some basic hardware items.

Make Hinges And Latches

You can use a nail or dowel coming from a frame into the swinging door as a latch. Or combine big staples and nails. You can also use pieces of inner tube, leather, or other flexible and durable substances, tacked on like hinges. Better yet, use a sliding door—a piece of plywood running between strips of wood—that doesn't need hinges. In parts of the country where wood is used for everything, like the Pacific Northwest, door and gate latches are made with wooden bolts sliding in wooden guides.

Make Clothes Hooks

If you have a wooden wall, or a wooden strip running along the wall, clothes hooks can be made easily by drilling holes in the wall and gluing in dowels or whittled sticks.

Make a Toilet-Paper Holder

You can make a toilet-paper holder out of a tree branch. Find a small Y-shaped branch. Carve it to shape and screw onto the wall. The same idea, but with a bigger stick, works for paper towels.

Make Handles

Lovely handles can be made using small, odd-shaped pieces of driftwood or weathered wood screwed into the front of the door or cupboard.

Make Curtain Rings

With a pair of pliers, you can improvise curtain rings out of clothes hangers. They can even be bent so they spring shut on the cloth. Generally, rings are better than sewing the cloth into a wide hem and then sticking the rod through; even if the hem is very big, it tends to bind, whereas a ring system slides easily.

Make Curtain Rod Supports

Curtain rods, shower rods, and towel-roll rods can be made from V-shaped supports by tacking two small pieces of wood to the wall.

24

Lower Heating Costs

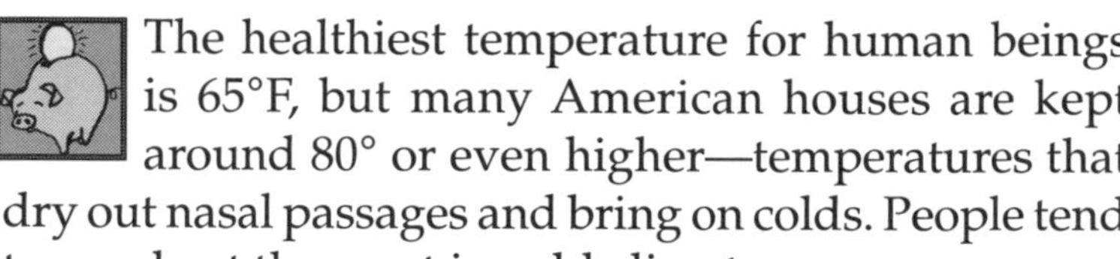

The healthiest temperature for human beings is 65°F, but many American houses are kept around 80° or even higher—temperatures that dry out nasal passages and bring on colds. People tend to overheat the most in cold climates.

Rather than overheating your home, put on a sweater, wear two shirts, or even wear long underwear. You'll save a great deal of money, because those extra degrees of heat are very expensive. Keep the thermostat set between 65F° and 70°F. Turn it down even lower at night. Get a down comforter, which can last for decades, and you'll be very cozy in bed.

Fix Radiators

Hot-water radiators sometime fill up with air; then the hot water can't get into them. Get a valve key from a hardware store and open the valve. The air will hiss out. When mostly water comes out, close it again. This may have to be done often, and if so, installing an automatic valve will cure the problem.

Steam radiators have a valve, which can clog. Turn off steam with the main turn-off handle. Unscrew the valve and clean out the hole with a piece of fine wire—a needle may work. Blow through or shake it, to get the water out.

Fix Gas Heaters

The most common trouble with gas heaters is that the pilot-light thermocouple, which generates current to run the thermostat and safety cutoff, is shot. Replacing it is not complicated, and good hardware stores sell replacements. Turn off the gas at the meter, then remove the thermocouple with a screwdriver and take it along to the store to be sure you get the right replacement.

Avoid Electric Heaters

Electricity costs far more than gas for a given amount of heat. But an electric heater may be justifiable if you want to heat one small room and leave the rest of the apartment or house cool. The most economical are the portable electric radiators, which are filled with fluid. They heat more slowly than the old fashion "space" heaters with the element that gets red when hot. Place the electric radiator under a window and keep it at a low setting. The slight coolness and draft around the window will cause the heat to slowly circulate throughout the room. Once warm, the heater is kept on continuously with very little energy.

Use the Stove

When all else fails, you can use the stove to heat your kitchen. Turn on the oven and leave its door open, with the broiler door open a crack. You also get quite a lot of heat if you turn on several burners and put big pots of water on them. The sides of the pots become heat radiators, and the water vapor from the boiling raises the humidity, which makes the air feel warmer, as in a steam room. If your stove is electric, this is a very expensive way to heat. However, if the weather is subzero, it may be life-threatening and stove heating can make a big difference.

Use a Wood Stove

Even in cities, wood for fuel is often available at prices that beat oil and gas per unit of heat——assuming, of course, that you have a really efficient stove and aren't just using a fireplace or an open Franklin-type stove. So if you love wood heat for its beauty or its odor, and don't mind doing the work involved, it's an attractive possibility. Don't use a fireplace, which is a net *loser* of heat—you suck more warm air out of the room and up the flue than the fire provides. Close the damper whenever you don't have a fire going.

Wood stoves use a renewable energy source. A good wood stove will warm an average-sized house quite satisfactorily if it is used right and is equipped with a blower or fan to circulate warm air to distant rooms. Sometimes ducting is better for this purpose. A good stove dealer will usually visit your house, recommend a stove appropriate to it, and give you the advice needed to run it correctly.

Before investing in a wood stove, explore the availability and price of firewood in your area. Lay in a supply of wood in the spring, so that the wood can be well-seasoned by the time you need it. Store it where rain or snow cannot dampen it. The best stoves burn modest-sized logs, so that the burning surfaces are at least half round—rather that split sides all around. Oak, hickory, and fruit woods give the most heat. You need some soft wood around to use as kindling in starting fires, of course. Green wood and soft woods should be burned only as last resorts because they give relatively small amounts of heat, and large amounts of creosote—which, sooner or later, you must clean out of your stove pipe and chimney.

If you live near woodland areas, having a chainsaw and pickup truck will enable you to gather your own firewood. Don't underestimate the sheer labor this involves, but it can reduce your fuel costs to very little. In national forests, with a permit, you can usually cut firewood for yourself. Write the Forest Service in care of the Department of Agriculture in Washington Dc for a brochure called *Firewood for Your Fireplace*.

Add a Greenhouse or Solarium

A greenhouse on your home will help heat your dwelling and provide you with a place to grow vegetables you can eat. If you're a high-rise dweller, you may have a balcony with southern exposure that you could convert into a greenhouse.

The greenhouse should be at the lowest level to allow heated air to rise through the house. To store heat efficiently, it must have a strong enough foundation to support earth-filled containers for plants as well as a concrete floor and a row of water-filled barrels. To control hot air movement and buildup, it must have ventilation openings to let outside air enter, and doors into the house living areas through which heated air can move. To prevent excessive heat in the summer, the greenhouse needs covering from shades, overhangs, or a deciduous tree, plus vents up high.

Even a small greenhouse can support a surprisingly productive vegetable garden. The plants help to humidify your air, which is especially healthful in winter.

Stop Air Leaks

Locate drafts—with a candle or burning incense stick—before cold weather comes, and fill the cracks. From the outside, use caulk, putty or sealing compound. From the inside, practically anything will do: torn up newspapers soaked in flour-and-water glue and tightly forced into cracks and painted when dry, or rags dipped in old paint and stuffed into cracks. Put weather stripping around doors so they close airtight. In cold country, some people cover the windows with sheet plastic.

Double windows, or even just plastic sheeting tacked over the windows, result in remarkable fuel savings. But perhaps the most important and easiest way to save money on heating and live a more stylish life is to wear a beautiful sweater and get used to an air temperature of around 68°F during the day and 55°F when sleeping. This is healthier for you, keeps the air from feeling so dry, and saves enormously on your utility bills. The same is true of air-conditioner cooling; try to get used to a 78F° level.

If you have a fireplace, make sure the damper shuts tight when it's not in use; if it won't, use a sheet of metal to cover the fireplace opening.

25

Cool Off Cheaply

In the Southwest, people use simple water-drip air coolers, sometimes called *in*, mounted at main windows or on the roof. These contraptions do not cool air as much as air conditioners, but they help a lot and are economical, whereas air conditioners can add $100 or more per month to your utility bill in the summer months and generate "processed" air that dries out your skin, hair, and nasal passages.

Sometimes one side of your dwelling faces the sun. This can be pleasant and a good source of solar-heating energy in the winter. In the summer, you might build an overhang of some kind as a shade from the sun. Consider putting up a bamboo shade or awning outside the windows, or pasting aluminum foil over the windows on the outside. Rubber cement holds pretty well if you clean the glass first and make sure to glue the edges down firmly. Large hardware stores like Home Depot and Orchard Supply Hardware sell special sun reflecting, shading film that you can put onto the window.

Use Fans

Hot weather can be made more tolerable by paying attention to the air circulation in your house, and by using a fan to circulate air to where it's needed. Houses cool down during the night, so keep your windows shut during the day and open at night. While you wait for your house to cool off in the evening, you might sit outside and listen to the noises of nature.

To use a fan to make air flow through a house, close all the windows but two: one where the fan is, and one at the other end of the house. Sometimes you get the best results with the fan in an upstairs room, pointing outward, and opening a first-floor window that's in the shade and not located over hot concrete.

Install Insulation

Many dwellings are not well-insulated, and in hot weather they can get unbearable which drives up your utilities in cooling the place. For both economic and ecological motives, any habitation that's likely to remain standing for more than ten years is well worth insulating. The result will be lower heating costs in cold weather and a more comfortable dwelling in hot weather—very possibly enabling you to avoid an energy-hogging and health-endangering air conditioner.

It's relatively easy to calculate the pay-off times of spending X dollars on insulating your ceiling or walls, which usually works out to be three to five years. Considering what else you might spend your money on, this is a highly profitable secure investment. Moreover, tax credits may be available and some utility companies will inspect your home and give you advice.

With insulation around the north side of a structure and large double-glass windows on the south side including insulating shutters to cover them at night, a house can get much of its space heating from the sun. This is especially true if the sunlight hits a large mass of concrete, stone, or water after it comes through the glass.

26

Reduce Utility Use

Utilities can be as much as 50% of the cost of running a household. There are a number of simple things you can do to greatly reduce this cost without sacrificing your quality of life.

Insulate Your Water Heater

Domestic water heaters accounts for more home energy consumption than anything but the furnace. Wrap the water heater with an insulation jacket from the hardware store. You'll cut heat losses by as much as 40%.

Your water heater will consume proportionately less energy, and do less environmental damage, if you use less hot water. Gas-burning water heaters and clothes dryers are far more economical to operate than electrical ones.

Turn off Stove Pilot Lights

You can save energy, and decrease ecological impacts, by eliminating pilot lights on gas stoves. They burn a surprising amount of gas, 24 hours a day. Matches or a mechanical or electric lighter are fine if you don't mind the trouble. New gas stoves come with electric lighters and these can be fitted into old stoves, but they have a significant breakdown rate.

Save Water

Even in rainy regions, water consumption has severe impacts on fish and stream bank life. Conserve it for both economic and ecological reasons. When shaving, brushing your teeth, and washing dishes, turn off faucets when you don't actually need them running.

Fix leaky faucet washers promptly; a slow drip can waste hundreds of gallons of water—besides making an annoying noise! Get a low-flow shower head. Ask your water company because they may give you one free. Or install a little disk called a flow restrictor in the shower head. Hardware or plumbing-supply stores sell them, usually for very little.

For decorative planting, choose species with low watering needs. For vegetables, plant closely in raised beds and use a drip watering system rather than overall spray watering. Cover exposed soil with mulch—which also minimizes pests. For lawns, minimize evaporation losses—and do your grass a favor—by periodic deep, long watering, in the evening or very early morning. Consider replacing some of your lawn with native plants. In washing your car, don't just let the water run; use a bucket of soapy water, and hose the car off only after you've scrubbed it.

Save Electricity

By turning lights off when nobody's using a room, not over lighting rooms, and avoiding high-wattage appliances like electric broilers, frying pans, hair-dryers, irons, and halogen torchière lamps, you can lower your bill substantially.

Of course, remembering to turn off the lights is always the problem, especially in rooms like the bathroom where a light could run for hours after use. An inexpensive way to put a stop to this is to install a chip-like device in the light socket , available in most hardware stores, which will automatically turn off the light after so many minutes.

Use Energy Saver Bulbs

The cost of lighting your dwelling is mostly in your electric bill, not in the cost of bulbs. During its 750-hour lifetime, an old-fashioned bulb eats up electricity worth more than five times what the bulb costs you. Compact fluorescents, though they cost more to purchase, save you money by lasting about ten times longer while using about a quarter of the electricity.

If you do buy standard bulbs, you get more light output from one 150-watt bulb than from two 75-watt bulbs. "Soft white" bulbs cost more and give less light. For hard-to-change fixtures, there are industrial bulbs that last 2000 hours. So-called "long-life" bulbs will cost you far more money in your electric bill than many early burnouts.

If conventional bulbs burn out too fast—especially if several of them burn out at once—it's probably because the voltage in your area surges above the standard 120 volts frequently. You may need to use bulbs rated for 125 volts instead of the standard 110, although they provide less light.

Tube fluorescents are even more efficient than compact ones, and they have better color balance, little flicker, and less hum if they have electronic ballasts.

Full-spectrum fluorescent tubes are available, and while they cost more, they have a pleasant—and healthier—color, close to sunlight.

Get "Lifeline" Rates

Most states require utilities to establish "lifeline" rates for those who have low income budgets and use little gas or electricity—especially older people living alone. The idea is that certain utilities, like gas, electric, and phone, are essential to maintain life. People on low incomes are provided these services at a reduced rate to maintain their "lifeline." If you live on a low-income, check with your utility company and make sure that you are getting this lower rate.

27

Fix It Yourself

Every household object you can make last longer saves you the cost of replacing it. Often a minor repair, which costs nothing except the use of a pair of pliers or some glue, will extend the life of an object for years.

Get Useful Tools

Every toolbox should be equipped with a full-sized hammer, small and medium screwdrivers, and pliers at the minimum. Also useful are: wood saw, pipe wrench, largish crescent wrench, medium-sized file, and hacksaw for cutting metal. Finally every home tool box should have several wood chisels, a putty knife, small paintbrush, and an oil can with lightweight oil.

You should also have several basic repair materials on hand. These include electrical tape and jars of assorted nails, screws, nuts, bolts, and washers. A box of spackle to patch holes in walls is good to have on hand along with a collection of several

kinds of glue. You should also have a spray can of silicone lubricant for sliding doors, windows, and drawers. A penetrating oil for unfreezing frozen nuts, locks, and hinges is also handy.

Rent Special Tools

Anything can be rented, from a small electric drill to heavy equipment such as a cement mixer. A few cities have free tool-lending "libraries."

Renting tools is better than owning them unless they're tools you use constantly. The more expensive the tool, the smarter it is to rent it. Often, being able to get the right kind of heavy tool will make the difference between being able to do a job yourself or having to hire a professional. Sanding and refinishing a floor is an example. You can rent a heavy sander for a day and do a job that would be impossible without it.

When you're checking out something from a rental outfit, be sure you know how to work it and that it's in working condition—otherwise you may be liable for repair costs. A good way to make sure of this is to ask them to show you how to use it.

Make a Large Work Area

The first thing you can do to make yourself more handy, is have or make a big surface on which you can lay parts out strictly in the order you remove them, and so far as possible in the relative positions they occupied. Second, you can code parts by marking them. For instance,when disassembling a gear mechanism, where worn teeth must meet just as before or they will bind, mark them by putting small punch marks on two teeth of one gear and on the tooth where they meet on the opposing gear. With wires, you can attach bits of colored yarn, or small pieces of masking tape with colored markings. With wooden objects, you can write corresponding key letters or numbers on the part of each piece where it meets another piece, so that in reassembling you bolt A back onto the other A, B onto B, and so forth.

How to Do Minor Repairs

Around every house there are things that drive you crazy because they won't work right.

Cabinets Don't Shut

Scrape off the bumps of paint that have accumulated around the edges of doors and around hinges and latch. Unscrew the catch and soak it in paint remover, or at least scrape it and squirt some penetrating oil into it. If the cabinet is no longer square, you may have to unscrew the hinges and plane the edges of the door.

Can Openers Won't Work

Soak the can opener in hot soapy water, then clean the working parts with an old toothbrush or toothpick. If the handle doesn't turn easily, put a drop of oil where the handle or shaft passes through the frame.

Bed Squeaks

Get rid of the springs—better for your body anyway. Lay plywood over the slats and sleep on that. If the frame of the bed squeaks, re-glue the loose joints. Or maybe do away with your bed entirely.

Electric Fan Doesn't Swivel

Clean the oscillating mechanism under the back of the fan with alcohol, paint thinner, or even soap and water. Put a little oil on the moving parts. Oil the fan motor—just a few drops—if you can find an oil hole.

Electric Iron Sticks

Irons get fouled from starch and soap residues. Washing it with soap and warm water when unplugged and cool will usually remove the stuff. Alternately, use very fine emery cloth or steel wool. After the iron is clean, coat it with candle wax or beeswax and wipe off the excess.

Burners Don't Light

Grease is probably the culprit. Clean the whole assembly thoroughly first—warm water and ammonia works. Poke a needle through all the gas passages. Adjust the pilot gas at the little screw on the gas tube. Remove the tubes to the burners and make sure they are clear and level. Sometimes blowing gently will light a stubborn burner. You'll save energy and money by using a laboratory-type lighter and turning the pilot light off for good.

Screen Door Bangs

Tack several layers of inner-tube strips along the door frame to cushion bang. You could also install a door closer or a snap-shut device that flips over as the door closes.

Problem Blinds

If you have roller shades, you should understand the clever little ratchet mechanism inside one end of the roller. A shade that won't stay down can usually be fixed by oiling that little ratchet. It has a spring that enables it to rewind the roller just as much as it's pulled down, no more and no less. If the shade is dropping loosely, you wind the spring up by pulling the shade down and then taking it out of the brackets and rolling it up to the top by hand. If it's snapping up too fast, do the reverse. Take it off the brackets and unroll it by hand. A shade that rubs against one of its brackets may not be mounted level, or you may be pulling it sideways as you reach for it. If the edges get frayed, trim them with a pair of scissors.

Electric Plug Falls Out

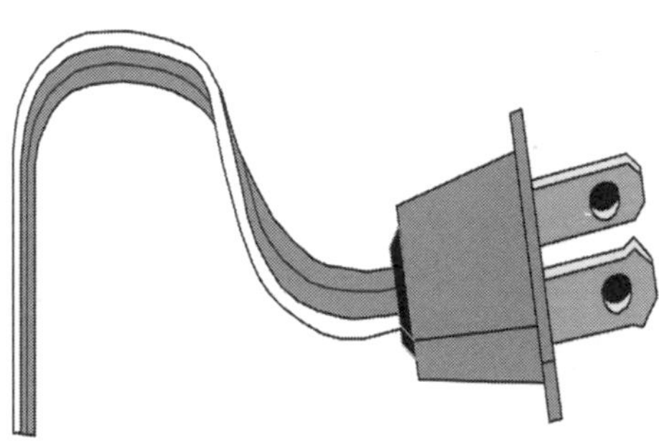

Sometimes you can get it to stay by bending the prongs of the plug outward slightly, and then reinserting it. In very old receptacles, however, you may need to replace the wall plug.

Electrical Trouble

When you move into a new place, make sure you locate the fuse box. The most common trouble with electricity is that a fuse or circuit breaker blows out because the circuit was overloaded with too many electric appliances turned on at once. If that happens, all the lights on that circuit will go out. If you have an old fashioned fuse box, keep a box of fuses on hand, since fuses almost always blow at night when stores are closed.

Turn off everything on the circuit, replace the fuse, then turn things on one by one, which can reveal a defective lamp or gadget. Often the circuit is overloaded and you have to unplug something.

Never put a penny into a fuse hole because that foils the purpose of having a fuse. If there's a short circuit in the walls, you may burn down the house. Replacing a fuse with a higher amperage one enables you to operate more lights or appliances but decreases the safety factor in your wiring. If your trouble is sudden surges of current from the starting up of a furnace or refrigerator motor, "delay" fuses will tolerate these surges without blowing. Resettable fusestats are also available.

Old houses tend to not have enough electrical outlets, so people get multireceptacle plugs to stick in them, and run extension cords all over the place. Don't run them under rugs, where foot traffic may wear through the wire insulation. Attach the wire to the baseboard as it goes around the room to keep it from getting mashed by shoes, furniture, and vacuum cleaners. Be sure not to puncture the wire.

Fix Small Electrical Appliances

Hot plates, waffle irons, toasters, hand irons, and hair dryers are all basically doing the same thing: heating the inside of some kind of case. They have a thermostat to keep them from getting overheated, and some have a fan to circulate the air they warm. Aside from cord trouble, the most common problem with these appliances is a break in the heating element. Over the years, the heating coils or strips get brittle, and a jolt may finally break them, so the current can't pass anymore.

The first step is to make sure that the problem is in the appliance and not the plug. Plug the appliance into another outlet. Check the prongs on the plug and the cord to see that the wire is okay. Next, open the appliance and see if you notice loose or disconnected wires. If you do, you can usually reattach them pretty easily.

Often the only problem with a lamp is a broken switch. If you take it to the home improvement store, a clerk can often show you what you need to fix it—which is usually something simple and cheap.

28

Fix Plumbing for Pennies

Many plumbing troubles are straightforward and can be fixed with simple tools and little money.

Open Clogged Sinks

Sinks and bathtubs have an S- or P-shaped drainpipe underneath, called a *trap,* in which a little water is retained to keep sewer gases from backing up through the drain into your house. They also trap grease from the dishwater and fat poured into the sink. When grease hits the cold pipes, it solidifies and then small pieces of food stick to it.

When a clog results, you'll need a *plunger*, sometimes called a "plumber's helper." It is a bell-shaped heavy rubber cup on the end of a wooden stick. Put the plunger over the drain, making sure it seals well, and work it up and down briskly. You'll hear gurgling noises in the drain, which means it's working. Stop and see if the water is going down. If it isn't, or is going down very slowly, do more plunging. When it does get draining better, run the water very hot for a while.

If this doesn't, the trap is so clogged with old material that the sucking and pressure of the plunger won't loosen it, or the obstruction is below the trap.

The next step is using a drain clearing chemical like Draino®. Generally, you pour about a cup full into the clogged drain and let it stand about 15 minutes, then flush with very hot water. Sometimes, you'll need to do this a few times to clear out grease and hair clogs. If the clog persists, then a professional plumber will be needed.

Clear Backed-Up Toilets

When your toilet backs up, first try the plunger. Put the seat up and get the plunger well set in the neck of the toilet bowl before you start plunging up and down with it. The obstruction is often within the toilet itself, not down in the drain pipes, so you have a good chance of dislodging it. More stubborn obstacles can be removed with a *snake* which is a long, thin, flexible cable that you gently twist and wangle down through the toilet. Short snakes can be purchased cheaply at a hardware store. Long snakes like the ones used by plumbers can be rented.

Stop Running Toilets

Running toilets really run up a water bill. Toilet tanks contain a valve operated by a float. When the tank has filled up, the valve shuts off the water. If it doesn't, the water won't turn off and the toilet will "run." Look inside the tank. Most likely the rubber tank stopper isn't fitting into its seal properly and it's allowing a little leak so that the water level never gets high enough to shut it off. Stoppers get flabby so they don't fit tightly anymore.The stopper can stick in the open position and not drop closed. New ones are very cheap. The brown deposits inside the tank are just mineral deposits from the clean, incoming tank water so don't worry about putting your hands into the tank.

Open Clogged Shower Heads

Water supplies contain minute quantities of minerals, and as the water runs through the fine holes in a shower head, some of these minerals get deposited. Old pipes flake off rust which can clog up the showerhead. To open a clogged showerhead, take off the faucet cover or showerhead, clean out rust bits and poke the holes open with a needle. While you're at it, install a flow-restrictor disk, which will save you a surprising amount on your water-heating bill.

Fix Leaking Faucets

Faucets knobs contain rubber disks called *washers* that press against a round seat to stop the water from flowing. Washers slowly wear out, causing the faucet to drip. They are easy and cheap to replace. Be sure you have turned off the water before unscrewing the packing nut at the top of the faucet. Use the shut-off valve under the sink or basin, or at the main house water-supply valve. Chances are that you won't be able to tell what size washer is needed until you get the faucet apart. Hardware and plumbing-supply stores sell little bags of assorted washers. Be careful to get the handle part screwed back in right, and don't tighten the nut more than is needed to stop seepage around the faucet stem.

When a faucet starts to leak, don't take to twisting it shut with force. That'll just wreck the washer and possibly its seat as well, which means a bigger repair bill because then the entire faucet assembly must be replaced. Make sure to replace washers as soon as you see signs of dripping because even a slow drip can waste an astounding amount of water.

29

Raise Children Cheaply with Love

Children are among the most interesting people you can meet, which you'll discover when you get to know a few. Many children are more fun to be with than adults—more cheerful, more ingenious, more enterprising, more playful, more affectionate, and more open. It's no accident that saints, artists, and other wise people have always paid attention to children. Children are naturally free spirited. They're full of energy. They're full of mystery and surprises. Children provide the immediate potential of the human race, so that in our little acts when interacting with them, we're shaping the freedom or the bondage of the next generation.

Buy Only Necessary Equipment

There's no question that having children is expensive. But the amount of money spent on nonessentials for babies is staggering. Inexperienced parents who wander into a baby-supply store are likely to come out with a ton of pink or blue "stuff" that neither they nor the baby need. Here are the essentials, much of which can be found in thrift shops, at garage sales, or from friends.

Bed

Vaudeville family children slept in their parents' traveling trunks. Trunks actually are not so good because they can accidentally flop shut and suffocate the baby. Dresser drawers and big boxes can serve as baby cribs. All they really need is four sides and something soft but flat—not a regular pillow—on the bottom.

Make a Cradle

Being able to rock the baby helps when it is fussy. You can suspend the sleeping place either by ropes or from some kind of bracket, like the beautiful old-fashioned cradles. A simple cradle can be made out of any box by putting rocker pieces at each end. With any of these ideas, you can attach a string to the thing and run it over your bed. A baby who wakes briefly can often be lulled back to sleep with a few tugs on the string—without your ever getting up. Since getting enough sleep is the number-one problem of new parents, such a device will richly repay the trouble it takes to rig up.

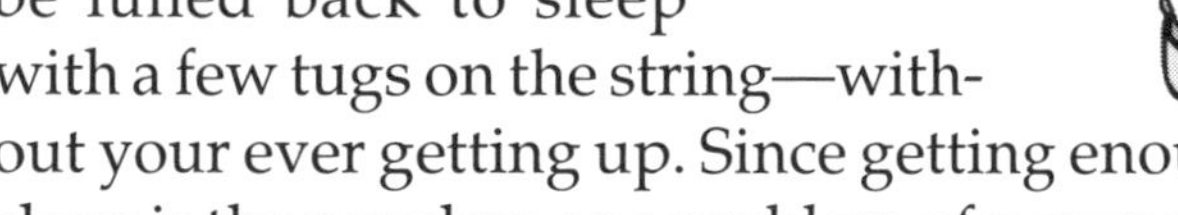

Improvise a Mattress Cover

The mattress needs covering with something totally waterproof. You can buy crib-size, waterproof sheeting that have flannel on both sides. It's washable, comfortable for the baby, and saves a lot of trouble. Pinned-down diapers work well as sheets when the baby is small. Make sure you have at least one very light blanket. Several light knitted or loosely woven layers are better than one heavy one.

Changing Table

You need a changing surface that enables you to change the baby smoothly, efficiently, and safely. The best is a dresser that's a comfortable kitchen-counter height. The area should be big enough so that an active older baby can't roll off. Pad the top with rags or cotton matting, and tack a heavy plastic covering over the whole thing. For comfort, lay a diaper or other washable cloth on top. Make an out-of-reach place to lay the diaper pins while they're off the baby so that the baby can't get a hold of one and swallow it. Sticking the pins into a bar of soap keeps them away from baby's mouth, in one place, and makes the pins easier to slide through the fabric.

Cloth diapers are much cheaper to use than disposable ones. They are also better ecologically. However, when traveling it's best to use disposable diapers.

Bathtub

A big plastic dish pan makes an excellent bathtub, and you can use it on the changing table, in the sink, or on the kitchen counter.

Clothes

In warm weather and in heated houses, babies don't really need much of a wardrobe. All that are needed are a couple of light shirts, a warm shirt or sweater, and several sleeper coveralls, which come in terry cloth and can be worn day or night, leaving the child free to move and warm. Sleeping sacks, which are nightgowns that have closed bottoms, are also useful. Such clothing is very inexpensive and readily available in second hand clothing stores, like the Goodwill and Salvation Army.

Improvise Playthings

Children follow a very simple rule about playthings. They imitate adults, in big things and in small, which is how they learn to be human. Young children love to play with pots and pans, for example.

The basic stock of toys that children need is simple, and can be improvised or picked up secondhand. Look for a store that recycles toys.

Balls

The simple fact that a ball rolls makes it entrancing to a baby. It makes little games possible for a two-year-old. And older kids can play a thousand games with a ball, any ball—a tennis ball, a Ping-Pong ball, a golf ball, a rubber ball, and blown-up plastic balls.

Dolls

If you're handy with sewing, you can make rag dolls and rag animals that will give your child a range of play fantasy. Some people are good at wood carving and can make special heads for dolls.

Blocks

Hardwood scraps from the saw table of a nearby lumber yard make good inexpensive blocks. Leave them in curious irregular shapes and just sand off the sharp corners. Real wood is beautiful; it feels and smells good. Wood blocks make an impressive sound when banged together.

Play Shelters

Children of all ages like to make little houses and tents for themselves. They can drape sheets or blankets over chairs and tables, or lean things against ropes you run across the room just above their head height. You can pick up used blankets and large curtains at thrift shops very cheaply. In fact, it is fun to take your child to the thrift store to pick out his or her own materials for constructing a play shelter.

Older children who can handle a hammer and nails should have scrap lumber available to them so that they can build more substantial huts outdoors. Tree houses, if you have good trees, are one of the best parts of childhood. Some parents build big play sculptures in their yards out of driftwood or salvaged timbers—you can let your imagination go, and the result will serve as a castle, a tower, a house, a store.

Buy Used CDs

Kids love to sing and dance around to lively music. There are many holiday music CDs available along with kids' stories. Large music stores often have a used section where they sell used CDs for less than half of the new price.

Improvise Art Materials

Children like to make things, and it gives them a sense of pride and competence. You should help them learn how to cut, paste, draw, and paint with materials that are easy to handle—things like paper, cardboard, Styrofoam®, and soft wood. Inexpensive basic materials include scissors, glue, poster paints, crayons, sticky tape, and a big sheet of oilcloth or plastic to lay over a table or on the floor, for the kids to work on.

For practically nothing, you can make dough modeling clay and it can be dried and then painted. Just mix flour and water and salt. The dough can be colored by mixing in a little food coloring.

Make Baby Food

Babies can and will eat all kinds of food if it is simply mashed soft enough for them. Often this can be done with a fork. With a food-processor or blender, however, you can mash up anything from asparagus to zucchini—even meat. Some adult foods, like applesauce, mashed potatoes, and scrambled eggs, are perfect for babies as is. Prepared baby food is one of the worst buys in the supermarket. Worse yet, some brands contain pesticide residues, and are loaded with sugar or salt.

30

Dress with Style Cheaply

Dressing cheaply with style is mostly a matter of having an open mind and using secondhand stores well. There are, however, many other ways to keep your clothing costs down.

Sew Clothes

Because of high fabric prices and the availability of inexpensive clothing in discount stores, sewing clothes is seldom cost-effective anymore. But a few sewing skills can be very handy in repairing clothes to make them last longer, or in making creative and stylish costumes for your kids. Such sewing is fun. Also, simple drapes or quilt covers that are very expensive in stores can be sewn quickly at home.

All you need for sewing, of course, is a needle, thread, and some scissors. A used sewing machine can be picked up cheaply and will probably last for decades. You'll also need a tape measure, a piece of chalk for marking cloth, straight pins, and an assortment of different colored threads which come in so many gorgeous colors that it's a pleasure to collect them. It helps to have a sewing box or basket with compartments to keep things in, because you'll begin to accumulate buttons, zippers, snaps, hooks, and other little objects.

Buy Durable Fabrics

By the time the goods reach the secondhand store, all their labels may have disappeared so you must rely on your feel for the material and the quality of workmanship.

Study Cloth

There is sleazy cloth and there is sound cloth. You can get a feel for the difference. Good material is essential for clothes to feel right. If your reaction to something is, "It might be all right for some occasions," take that as a danger sign. Really good clothes will make you feel right on practically any occasion. You can work in them, play in them, and even sleep in them.

The feel of fabric on your skin depends upon several factors. Here's another area where our incredible senses come into play, if we pay attention. If the fibers are hairy, like wool, it will feel warm. If the fibers are slick, like silk, rayon or nylon, it will feel cool—though silk cloth is actually warm. If the fibers are thick, the fabric will feel scratchy, as with coarse wool. If the fibers are fine and tightly woven, the fabric will feel smooth, as with good cottons and some synthetics. Ironing makes cloth feel cooler because it squashes down the fibers.

Hold the cloth up in a strong light and look at it very closely on both sides, to see how the threads run. Sunlight is best, since it shows true colors.

The warmth of a fabric depends on how much air it can trap among its fibers. Both thick and thin cloth is 60 to 90 percent air, and it is actually this air that keeps you warm. Wool, which has numerous tiny curly fibers, is the warmest, though some curlable synthetics are fairly warm. Warmth also depends on how well the fabric enables water vapor to evaporate from your body. Again wool is best. For outdoor activities, a sports-style fabric that "wicks" moisture away from your skin is well worth the money. For garments like winter coats, a wind-resistant outer layer over a thick, soft inner layer is the best combination. This can be achieved, for example, by a sweater and jacket, a quilted coat, or a zip-in-lining coat.

Buy Cotton

Cotton is washable, durable, and easily ironed. It mends and patches easily, and is available in every color conceivable; after long use, the colors fade to beautiful, subtle hues. Especially after some washing, cottons drape softly and are extremely good-feeling to the skin.

Buy Wool

More expensive than cotton and usually woven in heavier fabrics, wool comes either in plain or "worsted" form; the latter has more tightly twisted threads and wears much longer. Wool is also woven into loose-knit fabrics called jerseys, flannels, and cashmeres. Good woolen cloth is springy when you squash it and hard to wrinkle. As wool takes up moisture from body evaporation, it appears to generate heat. Unfortunately, wool has to be either hand-washed or dry-cleaned, and it's vulnerable to moths.

Buy Hemp

This extremely durable fiber was widely used in earlier times, and can be woven into many kinds of sturdy fabrics. Hemp is good for shirts or pants or backpacks that you expect to give hard wear. It's easy to wash and repair.

Be Selective With Synthetics

Many synthetics are useful supplements to the natural fibers, but they're seldom if ever as comfortable. People seeking to dress with durable style usually favor natural ones. In some garments, such as women's panties and panty hose, synthetics are positively undesirable, since they're not absorbent and concentrate heat and moisture.

Dye Fabrics

If you come across clothes that appeal to you in every way but their color, they can often be dyed. Hideous pinks can be turned into almost any dark color; pastels can be covered up. You can't obliterate flowery printed patterns and you can't turn a dark color into a light one, but there are a vast number of interesting transformations you can work on clothes. It's also fun to give color to items that are normally white, like undershirts.

Dime-store dyes don't take well, and they run onto your other clothes in the wash. Inquire at an art supply or hobby store for professional quality dyes. Natural dyes made from marigold and acacia flowers produce oranges and yellows. Dyes made from onion skins and coffee give a reddish brown. Generally, a lengthy soaking is required to extract color, and then the fabric must be simmered like a stew for an hour or so.

Fabrics, especially synthetics, dry a good deal lighter than they look when wet. Save the dye mix until your clothes dry; if they're not dark enough, put them in again.

You might try tie-dyeing, which was popular in the sixties. Bunch parts of the fabric together and tie them up tightly with string or elastic bands so that little or no dye can get into the tied up parts, which come out lighter. Since the whole thing involves many variables, you can't predict exactly what the results are going to be. The generally symmetric, vaguely circular motifs are always different, always subtle.

Delight in Patches

The patch is an ancient and honorable device and by no means a sign of disgrace. An honest, forthright patch is not a disfigurement but a decorative addition. Keep bright-colored pieces of cloth around, even if they're small. You never know when a shirt or skirt or pair of pants may wear through. Don't forget that patches can be laid over patches, too—and patches can be round or square or oval or oblong or star-shaped.

"Iron on" patches don't stay ironed on, and they're dull and standardized besides. Use strong, honest cloth, and sew it on carefully. Sew around the outer edge of the patch while turning it under neatly and around the edge of the hole or rip, so the fabric is firmly attached to the patch.

You can find beautiful fragments of cloth in the rag bins of secondhand stores. Let your imagination have free rein. The best patches are the boldest patches. When patching can no longer save the knees of pants, cut them off and turn the pants into shorts.

Replace Zippers

If zippers stick or don't run free, the tape on the back may be binding in the slider; sometimes you can iron it to stay out of the way, or tack it back with a few stitches. Dry cleaning can make a zipper run hard; sometimes rubbing soap on the teeth will lubricate it. The zipper is one of those rare modern inventions that's an indisputable improvement over its predecessor, the button. However, zippers do jam, they do pull off in time, and they do sometimes lose teeth. Then they need to be replaced. It is not as hard to replace a zipper as you may think, but you must get one that is the exact length of the old one. Carefully remove the old one by clipping the threads with a small knife or scissors, pin the new one in as you go—that way it'll be in place and ready to be sewn on when the old one is removed.

An alternative to zippers is Velcro®, which comes in strips sold at sewing stores. It's especially useful for fastening things like headbands and bicycle-light straps that need to be adjusted quickly.

31

Get Information Free and Fast

There are two major reasons for finding out things for yourself—entertainment and self-education. The more you enjoy learning, the more this distinction becomes happily blurred. When you settle for other people's answers, you get answers only to *their* questions, and not to the questions that are important to you. You'll do much better to find things out for yourself.

Use the Phone

With persistence and imagination, you can track down a vast amount of useful information on the telephone, thus saving walking, bus fares, and car rides. Don't hesitate to phone a store and ask if they have something you're looking for. When searching by phone, always ask each person you speak with for suggestions and phone numbers to pursue. Get the referring person's name because some times it helps to use the person's name.

Call Your Congressman

If you're trying to find out something that a federal office might be able to help with, look under "United States Government" in the first section of the phone book. If you get nowhere this way, phone the local office for your congressional representative who has a staff of people who know what the government does or doesn't do in your area, and may be able to give you individual names of people to call. The same goes for state, county, and city representatives. Your representatives need your vote, and maintain staffs that are supposed to keep you happy and thus get that vote; make them work for it!

Use Your Personal Network

People you know have a lot of information. Think of who among your acquaintances is most likely to have the information you are seeking. If he or she doesn't have the information, ask for a referral. Make sure you consider everyone you know, including the butcher, hair dresser, next door neighbor and so on. There's a statistic that shows that there are on average 5.5 referral links between any two people in the nation! When person A gives you the name of person B to call, that is one referral link. So if you keep at it you should find out what you need pretty quickly.

Use Libraries

Your library may be the single most important educational resource you have. You could never remember everything you may need to know; so you must learn how to find things out. Once you know how to find things in a library, you open up gigantic new frontiers of both knowledge and feeling.

Walking into a big library can be a little intimidating . Some libraries look like government offices, with huge pillars and lots of marble. But they're public institutions, open to all. Inside every library you'll find pretty much the same kind of arrangement, so that once you're familiar with its parts, you'll be able to use any library. Most libraries have public tours or other orientation sessions. Inquire at your local library. If there is no formal orientation, a librarian is usually happy to answer your questions and help you get started. In most cities, the reference librarian will take your questions about a particular book you are seeking by phone. If the library doesn't have the book you need, they can usually get it for you through interlibrary loan.

Read Periodicals and Newspapers

Because it takes about a year to publish a book, new information, especially of a technical or political nature, usually first appears in magazines. A taste for reading magazines can quickly get expensive. It's possible, of course, to stand at magazine racks reading for hours at a time until you get ousted. Visit the periodicals room in your library, where recent issues of many well-known and obscure magazines are available—often with comfortable chairs to sit in while reading. There is probably a magazine devoted to any subject you care about, from films to fortune-telling. Some are popular, with information ranging from the intensely useful to the purely commercial. A visit to a big university library periodicals room—which doesn't always require a library card— is an exhilarating experience with row upon row of highly specialized magazines, newsletters, and journal, in many languages.

The *Reader's Guide to Periodical Literature* indexes most of the major magazines, and tells which ones have printed articles in the last year on jet engines, capital punishment, genetic food alteration, Albert Einstein, or Susan B. Anthony. A reference librarian always has the *Reader's Guide* handy and can show you how to use it, along with more specialized similar guides in the arts, social sciences, and other fields.

Read Books

No matter where in the world you live, if you have access to a library, a bookstore, or the many new and used-book web sites on the internet, you can contact the finest minds humanity has produced. You can match your wits against truly original persons. It is in print that you can find really dissident, really critical opinions. Read to survive. Read to find out what's going on. Read for pure pleasure.

Enjoy Maps

Maps are both fascinating and endlessly useful. But you have to get the hang of reading them. It's a totally different process because it's visual. Maps can extend and intensify your world. It's awesome what you can find out from a map, even of an area you think you know pretty well. You find roads and streets you never knew were there, strange poetic names of places, and little hidden towns.

A useful tip: Lay out the map flat and orient its north toward the actual north.

In a library you can check into serious maps called *atlases*. Such maps show the altitude of places by a system of different colors for different elevations. They show major mountain peaks and tell how high they are. There may be special patterns to show which areas are forested and which are grassland. The best atlases are *The Times Survey Atlas of the World*, the *Rand McNally World Atlas*, and the *Reader's Digest Great World Atlas*. Sometimes you can pick up one of these in a secondhand store or at a yard sale, but most libraries have them.

The ultimate in maps of the United States is the series of super detailed topographic maps put out by the US Geological Survey. These cover sections of territory only a few miles across, but they show—in the country—literally every house, what the vegetation is like, whether streams are intermittent, whether roads are passable in winter, and so on. You can buy them from hiking equipment stores, special map stores, or by mail from the USGS. They have an index map that shows all their maps to make it easier to find what you need. USGS may be listed under "US Governmental Offices" in your phone book or try 800 information.

Internet web sites offer many kinds of maps, from elementary road maps to very sophisticated satellite-derived maps. You can find maps of driving routes and detailed lists of highways and streets to take to a specific destination.

Use the Internet

You don't have to have a computer and pay access charges to an Internet service provider company to use the Internet. Libraries, schools, and some bars and coffeeshops have computers you can use to access the Internet.

The World Wide Web, the liveliest part of the Internet, is something like an unimaginably vast library reference room with little organization and no librarians to control what's there. It accumulates stupendous amounts of authoritative information, wild ravings and fantasies, brilliant commentary, jillions of ads, and lots of cybersex. You quickly learn to pick your way through the web, to locate things that will really be useful and to spot junk when you see it.

Information—sometimes called "data"—cannot formulate or solve problems; only people with knowledge and ideas can do that. Information is plentiful, cheap, and useless in itself. Its value comes from somebody seeing something helpful, fun, or interesting that it can be used for.

Searching the Net

Information on the web is not like information in libraries, which is classified through an elaborate, long-established, and immensely useful system of categories. On the web, information is classified by "key words." For instance, if you wanted to find sites that deal with where robins live, you might ask your Internet browser to search for "robins +range." Unfortunately, if you do that, as I did when writing this passage, you find that there are 186,393 more or less relevant sites. When you look at the top few sites you realize that actually none of them are of any help. Very specific things are easier to find, but the sheer volume of stuff on the web is overwhelming. Even if you narrow down your search by using additional keywords, which is a demanding challenge, often the bulk of information is just too unwieldy to do anything with.

Electronic searching can be done within some web sites. For instance, go to the library website of a good university library and look for "robins +habitat." You'll find citations of both books and articles that can help.

32

Write Away for Stuff

One of the keys to enriching your life without spending much money is knowing how to reach out into the world and find out about things. Locally, you can do this by telephone, but writing letters is often necessary, too. It is important to write a letter so that it will work: bring back the information or response you want.

The first thing is to know to whom to write. If what you're after is information about a product, most sizable corporations have customer-relations departments to answer inquiries, and also web sites. If you have a complaint and don't know who ought to deal with it, write to "Office of the President" of the manufacturer. In writing to government offices, all that matters is to get the name of the office right.

Make sure you phrase your question clearly. Write your question in a way that invites a simple, clear answer. If you have a number of interconnected questions, put them in a numbered list. Whenever you're asking about something you may want to buy, ask for a price list and information about ordering.

Write your full name, address, and zip code at the top of your letter. Otherwise no reply can be sent to you. If a quick reply is important, you may get one by enclosing a postcard on which you've written your own name and address—that way the clerk who answers only has to jot down a reply on the card and drop it in the mail.

When you write a letter of complaint, describe the circumstances clearly and without name-calling. Close by saying exactly what you want: a refund, a replacement, a change of policy, or the disciplining of an unpleasant or incompetent employee.

What to Write for

There are many things you may want to write for. Government agencies—such as the Departments of Agriculture, Interior, or Health, Education, and Welfare—put out many free pamphlets. Bureaus in your state and local governments also issue useful items. Companies sometimes offer free samples. Publications often send you a sample copy in hopes you will subscribe. Organizations offering services or seeking your support will often send materials describing their work.

Locate Cheap Educational Resources

Education exchanges connect people who want to teach or learn about a particular subject. Workshop offerings range from technical matters like auto repair or computer programming to esoteric religious or health doctrines. Teachers range from bright, innovative, restless souls to incompetent characters. You're strictly on your own—you pay your money and take your chances, without benefit of accreditation machinery. The material offered may thus be far ahead of traditional university fare, out of date, or useless.

Community and city colleges cater to an interestingly varied student body, including people of different ages, work backgrounds, and motivations. Course units are considerably cheaper than at a university.

Universities offer extension courses where you can pick up skills and know-how fairly economically without having to enroll in a full time program. Many universities offer night and weekend classes in a wide variety of subjects—identical to university classes and available for academic credit. They're taught by people with good academic credentials, who have the same range of quality as professors. Extension divisions usually have correspondence courses, which are on a higher level than those offered by private correspondence schools.

Here's a tip: if you enroll in a class on a popular software program such as PhotoShop®, you can use your registration slip to purchase the software at a "educational discount" which is usually 50% off. With the high price of software that can be a considerable savings.

Many high schools offer night school or adult school classes—very economically—in vocational areas like auto shop or business and language skills. They also offer regular academic classes you can take to finish high school.

33

Find Free Fun

Much goes on in our cities that you can attend free—but most people never hear about it and end up watching television instead. There are also many free amusements that don't get listed anywhere; you have to find out about them on your own, depending on your tastes and ingenuity. For instance, many transit systems offer an all-day or all-weekend pass. With it, you can travel anywhere on their lines, especially way out to the ends, where the parks, beaches, and other interesting places are. Or you can ride around the inner city and get to know it better. Coastal and river cities have ferries that are cheap and fun. In general, anything that exists for everyday purposes can lend itself to inexpensive amusement. Think of yourself as a tourist visiting your own city—what should you take in?

Look in Newspapers

Sunday papers, community or special-interest papers, and some dailies have listings of free events like museums, special exhibitions, political meetings, lectures, plays, and concerts. Sometimes you can get in to events free by ushering. There are dances, movies, court sessions, and city council meetings, which are free or very cheap.

Read Bulletin Boards

These can be found in libraries, around universities and colleges, and sometimes in government buildings. Announcements of many coming events will be posted here.

Watch for Posters

Use of arty posters to announce rock concerts in San Francisco led to a new flowering of the art poster. Some cities provide kiosks where posters for concerts, plays, and other cultural events can be displayed.

Enjoy Parks

You can visit all the parks in your city, large and small. It's likely that some of them are really beautiful and interesting. For instance, botanical gardens have fantastic varieties of exotic plants. Or there may be an elegant rose garden, or a monster greenhouse where tropical plants grow and the air smells damp and strange. There may be a park with a lake where you can rent paddle boats, or where you can swim in the summertime. There might be a harbor park where you can look at the graceful boats. Walking or bicycling around a park can be relaxing. All of these adventures are free.

Most cities have free facilities of which few citizens are aware. There may be tennis and handball courts. There may be shuffleboard courts. Most cities have a public swimming pool with a small admission charge.

Neighborhoods

You can get a lot of pleasure out of your city just by walking around in places you don't usually go. In fact, that's one of the appeals of cities. There's a lot going on that you can see in a compact area. Don't confine yourself to the areas you're familiar with. Some of the most interesting areas are those inhabited chiefly by people from foreign lands: Chinatown, with its unique groceries and imported tourist goods; districts where there are Russian bakeries with exotic cookies and pastries; Black neighborhoods with African or Caribbean restaurants; Italian districts with extraordinary resources of pasta and delicatessen foods.

Find Cheap Movies

Movies seen at home are much cheaper than in the theaters, even when you spread the cost of the VCR out over time, and add in rental costs. Besides, you can make better popcorn, save money on theater refreshments, and invite friends to join you. Find a video store with an extensive stock—old films, documentaries, even experimental films.

Get Cable

Cable programming is a substantial monthly expense, even without subscribing to pay channels, but for a heavy consumer of visual material, it may be a good choice. Cable greatly expands access to video news and sports, as well as music videos. Cable will improve the TV's image so there are no reception problems. Some cable channels show films without commercial breaks, which is an immense pleasure.

34

Save on Legal Fees

Stylish living at any income level means taking care of essential business clearly and promptly so that your mind is free for more interesting things. With luck, you may have very little contact with legal matters during your life. But it's always possible that you'll be in an auto accident, get divorced, enter into a partnership, or even get arrested. It's certain that you'll die. All these events have serious legal issues associated with them that have to be taken care of correctly, or you can end up broke or in jail.

Luckily, self-help law advice is widely available, so that people can do many routine legal tasks for themselves without an attorney. These include writing wills, filing uncontested divorces, incorporating your business, changing your name, going to small claims court, patenting an invention, and dealing with immigration processes. Your library and bookstore probably have a whole shelf of authoritative books published by Nolo Press who publish self-help law books. They have an informative website which can be found by searching for "nolo". Nolo software is available to help you make out wills and certain other official documents.

Use Paralegals

Paralegals are a boon for ordinary people who can get legal work done at reasonable prices on issues including wills, bankruptcies, family legal matters, and restraining orders. When looking for a paralegal, find out how long they've been in business. If it's more than five years, they probably know what they're doing. Go check out their office. Paralegals are usually listed in the *Yellow Pages* under "Legal Typing Services," "Services for Attorneys," and sometimes "Divorce Assistance."

Check for Free Services

Neighborhood Legal Assistance services may help you if your income is low enough. Large counties also have County Legal Assistance offices to serve disadvantaged and unemployed people. In most states, the local bar association offers referrals to inexpensive legal advice. You can call the bar association in your area and request a referral to a lawyer specializing in your problem area. You are usually given names of three attorneys who will give you the first half hour of advice for a nominal fee.

If your income is less than 125% of the official federal poverty level, Legal Aid societies may be able to help. They can't deal with criminal charges, but they can help in "civil" matters such as rental disputes, child support and visitation rights, name changes, problems with banks or collection agencies, food stamps and Social Security, education, and immigration.

Don't Wait for a Crisis

Whenever a lawyer gets involved in a matter, it is going to cost you plenty. But there are times when you simply must have a lawyer. You need legal help if you are served with legal papers indicating that you are being sued; you are arrested for a crime; you are involved in an injury or property-damage claim; or you are involved in a contested divorce or one involving property or children.

Consider Mediation

Generally, the less you have to do with lawyers the better off you'll be. Many personal and neighborhood disputes can be settled through a mediation process—using a trained, impartial third party rather than risking the complications, expense, and bitterness of litigation. Many cities maintain dispute-resolution services, and there are also private organizations that provide mediators, which are listed in the *Yellow Pages*. People sometimes agree on a respected neutral member of their community, like a minister, to serve as mediator. In mediation, the objective is not so much to win as to restore peace and respect between you and your antagonist. This involves compromise and flexibility on both sides and can be very effective.

Even people with middle-class incomes often can't afford to undertake a legal action, because it costs more than they could expect to win. Besides, a trial—even if you're unquestionably in the right—is always a game of chance. The judge or jury may not believe you, despite the evidence. A good lawyer, who knows how to use threats and how to negotiate settlements, is often more effective than litigation—and a lot cheaper.

Get a Lawyer Beforehand

It's a good idea to establish a relationship with a lawyer before you really need one. Begin by asking around among your friends, including small business owners, for recommendations. Phone the local bar association and explain your situation and they'll send you the names of several attorneys active in the kind of work you need. Young, beginning attorneys may be the way to go if they're smart and eager. Having a small practice, they usually have more time for you. When you make a first appointment, ask for a reduced initial consultation fee.

Shop around for a lawyer—they're going to be your employee. You're hiring them. Some people suggest talking to five before choosing—though each consultation may cost you. Ask about their years of practice and what kinds of cases they've handled. Always be clear on the financial deal. Find out the hourly rates. It's often a good idea to pick one in the middle range of costs. Never be panicked into retaining a lawyer you don't feel comfortable about. Most legal emergencies can wait a few days. Examine the bill carefully. A company called Legalgard claims that 80 percent of legal bills contain "irregularities," and you can guess how often they're in your favor. Ethical lawyers never promise to win a case for you.

Negotiate Fees

Even just a half-hour discussion of your case with a lawyer will cost something, since most lawyers don't give free advice.

Sometimes layers will take a case on "contingency," especially personal-injury cases. In this arrangement, if the lawyer wins, he or she pockets a third to a half of the "award." If the case is lost, the lawyer is not paid and you aren't out anything at all. Make sure your liability for court costs is defined in a written agreement with the lawyer. You can negotiate a "cap" on a lawyer's fees, incidentally.

You can often dicker with a lawyer to go down in the fee. A few lawyers practice in prepaid groups the way doctors do. This promises better and cheaper legal service. Check the *Yellow Pages* or the Internet for listings.

Beware of "legal clinics." If sponsored by a law school, they may indeed be a low-cost clinic. Others are simply law offices specializing in easy, standard jobs like uncontested divorces but charging high fees for everything else.

Use Small Claims Court

This is a special court where claims involving small amounts—usually up to $5,000—are decided. A lawyer can not represent you and you can't appeal if you lose—though the person you sue can appeal if he or she loses. Small claims court is cheap, easy, and quick. If you have a good case with good records and good witnesses, you're likely to win.

If you decide on small claims court, you should then send a certified letter to the person or company you plan to sue, stating your case and informing them of your plan to sue if they don't give satisfaction within a set period, typically 5-10 business days. Most court jurisdictions have an arrangement with local attorneys or paralegals to provide free legal advice to people planning on using small claims court to settle disputes. Another resource is the Nolo Press book, *Small Claims Court*.

What to Do

Prepare for your appearance by getting together relevant documents such as work orders, purchase orders, canceled checks, written estimates. Jot down an outline of your story, with dates, so you will have it straight when telling the judge. Bring along any objects that might be useful in making your case, such as damaged items and witnesses who can support your story. An auto mechanic makes the best witness in suing a repair shop, for example. Sometimes you can get an expert, like an auto mechanic, to write a statement about the condition of your car. Alternatively, people often get several bids for the cost of a disputed repair to present as evidence. Get to the court early. Watching how other cases are handled can be helpful.

The judge will ask you to describe your side of the argument and why you think you're entitled to payment by the other party. State your case factually and avoid making emotional accusations. It helps to not look at your opponent while you're talking. Present your story logically and as briefly as possible. Then your opponent will have the chance to answer your charges. The judge usually asks you and your opponent questions to clarify the issues. Typically, you get the judge's decision by mail.

If you win, the losing party usually pays up immediately. If not, you might have to get a court "writ"—a legal paper that forces the loser to pay.

Pursuing a case in small claims court will cost you a small fee and time away from work. But it is far less than a lawyer would charge. Landlords and storekeepers can also sue you in small-claims court. If that happens, you must show up on the appointed day in court or you will lose the case automatically.

35

Use the Green Triangle

Living an ecologically sensible life brings a richer, more interesting, fuller, longer, less stressful, and healthier life. Ecologically conscious "light living" makes sense for anybody who is seeking a more meaningful way to relate to money and work.

The Green Triangle

The three points of the Green Triangle are environment, health, and money. *Anytime you do something beneficial for one of them, you will almost inevitably also do something beneficial for the other two*—whether you're aiming to or not.

Health

Suppose you decide to improve your health by eating less fat-filled meat and dairy products and more vegetables and fruits. This will decrease your chance of heart and artery disease and prolong your life. Since meat and dairy products are relatively expensive, you'll also save quite a bit of money. Moreover, you'll help the environment—since meat production is a very land-intensive and resource-consuming use of our farm productive capacities.

Environment

Let's assume you do something beneficial for the environment, like walking or bicycling instead of driving. You cut down pollution emissions, you reduce smog and lung damage, you decrease acid rain, you decrease the damage caused to the Earth by mining ore, smelting it, and fabricating and transporting car components. You decrease global warming. And you help your health, because you get more regular exercise, and you save money on gas, oil, and car depreciation.

Money

The third point of the Green Triangle is just as potent. Anytime you do something beneficial for your pocketbook, like not buying an expensive gizmo whose manufacturing expends a lot of energy and uses a lot of raw materials, or by not taking a car trip that turns a lot of petroleum into atmospheric pollution and noise, you help the Earth. You probably also do your health a favor, since you're less stressed out by not having to earn the money to pay off the gizmo or trip.

In addition, not pouring emotional energy into caring for, repairing, or protecting the gizmo leaves time and attention for other human beings and the kind of spontaneous improvisation and fooling around that our species evolved to be good at.

Everyday Applications

When you apply the Green Triangle to your everyday life, examples of delightful synergistic effects can be found everywhere. For example, low- or no-cost fun with other people is almost always more ecologically and financially desirable than hard work and heavy consumption. Exchanges outside the cash economy—trading massages, for instance, or passing on extra garden vegetables, knowing your neighbor will probably someday help you with a carpentry problem—don't have monetary ramifications you have to worry about. Growing or making your own is usually cheaper and healthier, as well as more ecologically benign.

Go Triangulate!

Remember that there is no such thing as totally innocent purchasing, even in countries with eco-labeling programs that guide consumers to less-damaging products. However, the *really* ecologically damaging things we do are to use cars, eat meat, have more than one child per parent, and live in separate single-family dwellings—apartment living is something like five times more energy- and materials-efficient.

The Green Principle

The underlying green principle is: *buy less.* Odd as it may seem, the simple act of consuming less is probably the most radical step you can personally take to save the Earth. Watch for the next Buy Nothing Day—the day after Thanksgiving. Joining in will open your eyes to how much of your energy is locked up in buying.

Index

D

E

U

V

W

Y

Z